I0150575

BOY SCOUTS

IN
MAHONING
COUNTY

1911 - 1993

TONY VALLEY JR.

Life is not about accomplishments.

Life is about the journey you take along the way.

Books have been provided for several Mahoning County Public Libraries and the Mahoning Valley Historical Society.

First Edition, First Printing: April 1993 - Limited Edition of 135 numbered books

Second Printing: June 1993 - 100 books

Second Edition: March 2010

ISBN 978-0-9826847-0-2

Published and Copyright © by Tony Valley Jr., April 1993, February 2010
All rights reserved.

No part of this book may be reproduced in any form whatsoever, including mechanically, electronically, digitally or photographically, without the written permission from the author. This book was produced solely and in its entirety by the author including research, interviews, writing, typesetting, reproduction of photographs, layout, paste-up and printing.

This book is about: Mahoning Valley Council
Boy Scouts of America
3712 Leffingwell Road
Canfield, Ohio 44406

Photo on front cover: Scout is unknown, circa 1920's.

CONTENTS

SECTION I

Scout Unknown
1925

DEDICATION

A Scout's values and character begins at home with teachings from the parents.

Therefore, this book is dedicated to my parents for their love and total support of my involvement in Scouting throughout the years, and for encouraging the completion of this book.

photo by Jack Acri

Tony and Dorothy Valley, Sr.

ACKNOWLEDGEMENTS

When I first contemplated researching and writing this book in 1984, I thought it would be an easy task! I had what was considered to be the largest collection of pictures, documents and other information on this subject known to exist. I have spent countless hours and money over the past eight years working on this project.

The fascinating material you are about to view could not have been presented without the cooperation of the many people who contributed freely of their time and knowledge, and in some cases opened their personal archives to me during the interviews with them. Their cooperation greatly assisted the effort to make this the foremost authoritative text ever compiled on the "Boy Scouts in Mahoning County".

Special thanks are in order to the following people: Jack Acri, professional photographer and friend who has donated his services to me on many occasions; Joe Angelo Sr, close Scouting and backpacking friend for many years; Fred Baird, Council Executive and long time close friend. We've spent many quality hours working and talking together over the years. Fred supported this project totally and offered any assistance that I needed; James L. Beeghly, Council President from 1957 to 1960; Nancy Bokesch, Council Accounting Specialist; Mike Bogan, as a Scout in 1927 he was selected to place a wreath on Henry Stambaugh's grave; Kay Bozman, the daughter of Karl Granger; Edward Cook, Richard Cook's father, provided several albums of photos that he photographed as a Scout in the early 1930s; Wilbur Dimit, photographed 16mm black/white movies of Scouting activities in the 1930s; Jeff Dyer, Scouting and trek partner for many years, provided photos and allowed his collection of memorabilia to be photographed; Mike Dyer, responsible for saving several rolls of black/white 16mm film from the trash at the council office on Rayen Avenue; Janet Walker Filban, Harry Walker's daughter; Florian Ernst, helped build the Hoover Cabin as a Scout; Mrs. Ladonna Frondorf, provided a photo of Harry Walker; Randy Geho, long time close friend, for the drawing on page 80; Karl Granger, Scoutmaster of Troop 44. He rode a horse in his younger days. Rumor had it that when his horse died he buried it under a large rock in Poland Park! Mr. Granger died in 1987 before his 101 birthday; Earl Hensel, allowed me to photograph two books that were written by first Council Executive Conrad Meinecke. One of the books illustrated the "Chief's Lodge" that he helped build on the north bank of Indian Creek in Camp Stambaugh; Sue Hoffman, for her leads; Bart Ingram; mentor and long time close friend, District Executive, and Camp Director in the late 1960s and early 1970s, Bart and I share many memories of camp and Scouting together; Mrs. Henry Verda Katschke, wife of Henry Katschke who was Council Executive from 1949 to 1968. Verda Katschke donated Henry's personal scrap books, movie film, and uniform pins; Bobby Kneen, while in the Order of the Arrow in 1967, Bobby and I collected some history on Camp Stambaugh; Robert H. Lohrman, helped build the Hoover Cabin in the late 1920s; Joe Majzic, for the deal on screening photographs; Brian Massucci & Kurtis Smith, for their cooperation at Kinko's; Henry and Violet McNatt, provided articles written by Violet in "The Sebring Times" in 1979; Don and Gladys Mikkelson, long time friends, provided photos and many interviews with Don while walking through camp. Don served as Camp Ranger from 1955 to 1980. Gladys served as camp cook for many years, and both lived on camp property, we also have fond memories of camp together; Walter Payne, stated during our interview that the first Negro Eagle Scout in our council was in 1935; Hank Perkins, Chief Photographer while working for WFMJ Television, made a video tape documentary on Camp Stambaugh in 1973; Penny Shaffer, council registrar; Karl Schwab, Vindicator newspaper columnist provided copies of index cards for Scouting articles; Henry Sforza; long time friend, provided Catholic Committee information; Ray and Jean Slaven, long time friends, provided photographs; Thetas Smith, retired council bookkeeper; Mitch Stanley, wrote the story for the 1973 video tape documentary on Camp Stambaugh that was aired on WFMJ television; John Wallis, brother to Lloyd Wallis whom the Wallis Lodge is named after. John was also a member of the Council Executive Board. He provided photos dating back to 1914; Dale Wegele, a Scout of Karl Granger's; John Wolboldt; loyal friend who is always there when I need him. He also provided countless hours of Scouting stories.

Others deserving of thanks are: The Mahoning Valley Historical Society, for allowing me to research their files; The Youngstown Reuben-McMillan Public Library, where countless hours, days and months were spent viewing microfilm of unindexed newspaper dating back to 1910...page-by-page!; Scouting Magazine, for National Scouting information; The 1959 Book of Scouting, for the Baden Powell story and Scouting Comes To America information; and the 1945 Boy Scout Handbook, for the illustrations.

More photograph credits: Lee Banks, professional 1950s-1960s; Dale Beckman; Jim Driscoll Sr; Ed Enterline; Ernest E. Grass, professional 1950s; A.D Hamilton; Bud Harnishfeger; Hart & McCarthy, professional 1920s; Robert Manchester; Butch Maro; Milt Revzin, professional 1930s; Tony Ricci, professional; Paul Schell, professional 1950s-1960s; Spratt Studio, professional 1950s; Jerry Stanovcak; Nick Valley; Tony Valley Sr; Vindicator and Telegram Newspaper; and Marty Wendt.

Finally, I would like to thank my parents to whom this work is dedicated for their encouragement and financial support in this project, and to all of the others, too many to mention, for their help and confidence.

FORWARD

by FREDERICK L. BAIRD
COUNCIL EXECUTIVE

It might be said that this book is the result of a self imposed mandate to preserve the past as well as more carefully record the events of the day.

Those who know him best refer to Tony Valley as a walking encyclopedia of information about Scouting in the greater Youngstown, Ohio area.

Those who have read his writings remember them as carefully crafted accounts of important events, coaxed from what is now dry, fragile, musty smelling parchment-like paper, reluctantly yielding to his persistant research, to become captured forever in his word processor and ultimately brought together in this book. This work will be given a place of prominence in many a Scouter's library. Young and old alike will often slowly turn its pages.

With Tony's keen interest in the history of Mahoning Valley Council, Boy Scouts of America, he has caught the attention of many Scouters with his meticulously researched and incisive accounts of events that were all but lost.

But this book is more than a labor of love. It is the result of a burning conviction that we can learn from the past and in so doing we can help shape the future.

It has been my privilege to know Tony as a friend. I have enjoyed listening to and sharing with him while he was researching and bringing this material together. On the subject of Council history, he speaks and writes with a passion and a clarity that gives fresh new meaning to the events of the past.

Frederick L. Baird
Council Executive

INTRODUCTION

The Scouting you will read about has endured the test of time and survived many changes. The photographs and illustrations are exciting and offer an opportunity to step into the past. You will see how the Boy Scouts in Mahoning County looked from their beginning in 1911 and you will follow their growth and changes into 1993. This book has something to say and much to give to every generation who reads it.

I started working on this book in 1984 because I felt new Scouts and leaders should know about Scoutings past in Mahoning County. Many of the great Scouters that I grew up with and learned from while I was a young Scout were moving on to the great Scoutmaster in the sky. I wanted to preserve some of their past. In the process of researching and interviewing, I became more and more involved in the exciting people and events of our council's history. With 82 years of information and photographs to draw from, where do I stop?

We learn from the past, our own past and the past of others before us. This is why our history is a precious resource. We should do all that we can to preserve it, and to ensure its accuracy so it can be passed on from one generation to the next.

Let our history serve as a REMINDER of where we came from. Let it serve as a TESTIMONY of what we can accomplish. And, let it serve as a TEACHER of what we can do for others when we work together.

This book is a result of those people who are concerned for Scouting's future as well as Scouting's past.

Some of the great developers and leaders of Youngstown such as the Stambaughs, the Wicks, the Butlers, and many others, were there in our council's beginning helping to carve its future. The success of this program throughout its 82 years in Mahoning County is a result of devoted commitment of tens of thousands of concerned people. It would be impossible to include every person and activity in this book.

The outdoors has always been the class room for the Scouting program. Scout camps like our own Camp Stambaugh give young people a chance to find themselves and give stability. Scout camps create an environment for teamwork and leadership, while helping in the development of a value system.

When we teach others, we should remember to not only teach "What" they should do, but we must teach "How" to do it, and give sound reasons "Why".

As you read this book, keep time in perspective. How we live today in no way resembles how it was in 1911.

What I have learned most from working on this book is that we are mortal and possess a limited amount of time on this earth. I've interviewed Scouters in their 80's and 90's who shared childhood photos of themselves and friends. Many of whom have passed on since.

One interview comes to mind. An elderly Scouter called me on the telephone and wanted to meet with me. He heard that I was working on this book and he had some photos and stories to share. I responded that I would meet with him the following week. He said, "I may only have tomorrow Tony". I'm sure at the time he was joking. But I agreed to meet with him the next day. Of the photos he gave me, one was of him and his fellow Scouts at age 14 dating back to 1916. I studied the photo closely and then looked up at him. I looked back at the photo and then looked up at him again. Realizing the expression on my face, he replied, "You're going to get old too some day Tony." Why has that remained in my mind, you ask! He passed away shortly after, and he was right. I'm going to get old too some day, and then pass on. So are you! It made me realize even more, how important it was to finish this book, and any other "burning desires" I have in this life.

Many people are so in a hurry to live, that they don't find time to plan their course in life. But time flies by forcing them through life whether they are ready or not. Some become successful. Some just exist, waiting for external changes before they will make internal decisions. And others wander around aimlessly like a sailboat without a rudder. Some of the wanderers make it through life unscathed, while the unlucky ones fall short of any dreams at all. ...time waits for no one, and there is much to do, so enjoy life.

As you move on to the following pages, you will relive some of the great adventures in Scouting of yesteryear in Mahoning County.

SECTION II

Colonel Robert Baden Powell
at Mafeking in 1899.

BADEN POWELL, The Founder Of Boy Scouts

Robert Stephenson Smyth Baden Powell was born in London, England on George Washington's 125th birthday February 22, 1857. He was the fifth son and eighth child of H.G. Baden Powell and Henrietta Smyth. His father was a man of many talents - clergyman, naturalist, and professor at Oxford University. His mother was the daughter of the British admiral W.H. Smyth.

Robert never knew his father well. He died when Robert was only three, leaving his mother to raise nine children. "How that wonderful woman managed to bring us all up," said Baden Powell many years later, "I do not know and cannot understand. It was her influence that guided me through life...".

As a boy, Robert Baden Powell lived an active outdoor life with his brothers. He loved nature, hunting and outdoor living. At 13, he entered Charterhouse School. He was not a smart student. One of his school reports read: "In mathematics he appears to have lost interest in the study; during French he frequently seems to fall asleep." But he was a popular pupil.

Robert spent many of happiest hours at Charterhouse in "The Copse," a wooded area outside the school grounds which was off limits to the students. Here he taught himself to snare rabbits and cook them over an open fire. He kept the fire very small so that the smoke would not give him away. He also learned the use of woodsman tools, to follow tracks of wild animals and to study nature. These skills became of great use to him in later life.

While on school vacations he joined his four brothers in outdoor activities such as paddling up the Thames River, hiking in Wales and Scotland, and boating along the English coast.

When Baden Powell graduated from Charterhouse, the British Army was recruiting men for an open examination for commissions as officers. Robert took the examination and of 700 candidates he finished second. The great demand for officers for overseas duty led Robert in 1875 at the age of 19 to join the British Army. He was commissioned as sub-lieutenant and went to India. He became committed to soldiering. He was very good at scouting and surveying on expeditions into the wild northwestern part of the country.

By 1885, after eight years service in India, Baden Powell was a captain.

In 1887, Baden Powell's uncle, General Sir Henry Smyth, was made commanding officer of British South Africa. He invited his nephew to join him as his aide. B.P. jumped at the opportunity and immediately sailed for Cape Town. Soon after his arrival, one of the Zulu tribes to the north rose in rebellion against the British. Baden Powell was appointed staff officer for the forces sent in to stop the uprising. The rebellious Zulu chief, Dinizulu, quickly gave up the fight. A long necklace of wooden beads was captured from Chief Dinizulu. Baden Powell was now a Major.

Baden Powell was assigned to the whole Mediterranean area and served as a spy in Austria, Italy, Albania, Turkey and other countries of southern Europe.

In 1895, Baden Powell returned to Africa. Differences in South Africa between the British government and the Boers of the Transvaal and Orange Free State had reached the breaking point. War seemed inevitable. Now a Colonel, Baden Powell was ordered to raise two battalions of Mounted Rifles and proceed to the town of Mafeking, an important railroad center close to the Transvaal border.

Baden Powell became exasperated with the inability of city bred recruits to exist comfortably in wild mountainous country. So to train them, he worked out a series of games and activities to make his men physically strong, self-reliant and able to live comfortably in the wilderness. The men enjoyed these games and quickly became skilled.

The Boers declared war on October 1, 1899. Mafeking was immediately attacked. Every able bodied man in town was made part of the defending force. Even the boys signed up and were put into a special cadet corps as bicycle messengers.

For 217 days, Baden Powell and his force of less than a thousand held out against an enemy force ten times as large until British relief forces fought their way in on May 17, 1900.

Great Britain had been holding its breath through these long months. When the news finally came, "Mafeking has been relieved!", Great Britain went wild with joy.

The name of Baden Powell was known to all. Queen Victoria made the defender of

Mafeking, the youngest Major General in the British Army at age 43.

During the time Baden Powell was training his men, he wrote a small book called, "Aids to Scouting", outlining some of the basic skills required of a soldier who explored and searched enemy territory to obtain information. Baden Powell illustrated the manuscript with his own drawings and later sent it to a London publisher. His fame had led boys to read and use the book.

Baden Powell saw a great challenge in this. If a book for men on scouting practices could appeal to boys and inspire them into action, what would a similar book written for boys do!

He decided to make use of his fame to help British boys become better men. He developed his ideas. Based them on his own experiences as a boy in England and a soldier in India and Africa. He then tested them with 20 boys by holding the worlds first Boy Scout Camp on Brownsea Island in Poole Harbor, England in August, 1907. On May 1st in 1908, Baden Powell published the first Boy Scout book called, "Scouting For Boys". It became an instant best seller. Scout patrols sprang up in England and soon after in many other countries. By 1910 the movement had grown so large that Baden Powell felt it necessary to sacrifice his army career to dedicate the rest of his life to Scouting.

Robert Stephenson Smyth Baden Powell was his full name. He is sometimes referred to as B.P.

B.P. was a soldier, artist and an author. He was an officer with the British Army in India and Africa. He had been at various times in his military career a polo champion, a big game hunter, a tamer of wild horses, and a spy for the British Army in Russia, Greece, Turkey and Italy.

The day the Scouting movement reached it's 21st birthday, King George V of England honored B.P. by making him a Baron under the name of Lord Baden Powell of Gilwell.

During the remaining years of his life, Baden Powell traveled around the world to encourage the spread of Scouting. In 1920 he called Scouts from all nations where the movement had taken root to the first World Jamboree in London. Here B.P. was acclaimed "Chief Scout of the World." Other World Jamborees followed: 1925 in Denmark, 1929 in England, 1933 in Hungary, and 1937 in Holland.

At age 81 he went to Nairobi, Kenya Africa with his wife to spend his last days in the country he loved so well. There he died on January 8, 1941 and was buried in Kenya.

Lord Baden Powell left the following Farewell Message at the 5th World Jamboree in Holland in 1937:

BADEN POWELL'S FAREWELL MESSAGE

"Dear Scouts,

If you have ever seen the play 'Peter Pan' you will remember how the pirate chief was always making his dying speech because he was afraid that possibly when the time came for him to die, he might not have time to get it off his chest. It is much the same with me, and so, although I am not at this moment dying, I shall be doing so on one of these days and I want to send you a parting word of good-bye.
Remember, it is the last you will ever hear from me, so think it over.
I have had a most happy life, and I want each one of you to have as happy a life, too.
I believe that God put us in this jolly world to be happy and to enjoy life. Happiness doesn't come from being rich, nor merely from being successful in your career, nor by self-indulgence. One step towards happiness is to make yourself healthy and strong while you are a boy, so that you can be useful and so you can enjoy life when you are a man.
Nature study will show you how full of beautiful and wonderful things God has made the world for you to enjoy. Be contented with what you have got and make the best of it. Look on the bright side of things instead of the gloomy one.
But the real way to get happiness is by giving out happiness to other people. Try and leave this world a little better than you found it, and when your turn comes to die, you can die happy in feeling that at any rate you have not wasted your time but have done your best. 'Be Prepared' in this way, to live happy and to die happy - stick to your Scout promise always - even after you have ceased to be a boy - and God help you to do it.

Your friend,

Baden Powell"

SCOUTING COMES TO AMERICA

It was on a very foggy day in the fall of 1909, that <u>William D. Boyce</u>, a 51 year old American publisher from Chicago, Illinois was having trouble finding his way around London. All day long the city had been covered with heavy fog. Street lights had been turned on before noon. Now night was coming on and it was almost impossible for the stranger to find his way. He stepped under a street lamp to locate himself when out of the gloom a boy approached him dressed in a wide brimmed hat and short pants and asked if he might be of service. The publisher gladly accepted the boy's offer. He told the boy where he wanted to go and was surprised when the boy saluted him and said "Come with me, sir".

Upon reaching his destination Mr. Boyce reached into his pocket and offered the boy a tip. Boyce was more surprised than ever when the boy refused it. The boy said "No thank you sir, I am a Scout. Scouts do not accept tips for Good Turns".

"Good Turns? Scouts?" asked Mr. Boyce, "What are Scouts?" The boy told the American about Scouting. Boyce was very much interested and wanted to learn more. He had the boy take him to the headquarters of the British Boy Scouts. When they arrived at the headquarters, the boy disappeared into the fog. He has been known ever since as the <u>"Unknown Scout"</u>.

At the headquarters Boyce met Baden Powell and became very impressed with Boy Scouts. Boyce had many dealings with boys through his business enterprises, but none of them had ever struck him as forcibly as his first encounter with a Boy Scout. Boyce was determined that American boys should have the great game of Scouting, so he brought Scouting back to America. He carried with him Scout literature, uniforms, and insignias. As soon as he arrived home, he introduced the Boy Scout idea to America. He worked with his friend, Colin H. Livingstone and other people in Washington, D.C., and with them established a new corporation called:

<u>"BOY SCOUTS OF AMERICA"</u>
<u>February 8, 1910</u>

Ever since then, February 8, 1910 has been known as the birthday of Scouting in the United States. One Good Turn to one man became a Good Turn to millions of American boys. Such is the power of the Good Turn.

Seventeen years after the unknown Scout had done his good turn, the boy who wanted nothing for himself received the highest award the Boy Scouts of America has to offer, the <u>Silver Buffalo</u> which is presented for distinguished service to boyhood.

The Silver Buffalo award is a small replica of an American buffalo, suspended from a white and red ribbon around the recipient's neck. For the unknown Scout, his award took the shape of a large bronze cast of a buffalo mounted on a wooden pedestal, erected at the International Boy Scout Training Center at Gilwell Park, England.

The boy himself was not there for the ceremony because he was never found. The plaque on the pedestal read:

"To the Unknown Scout whose faithfulness
in the performance of the 'Daily Good Turn'
brought the Scout movement to the
United States of America".

William D. Boyce was not the only American who had become convinced of the importance of Scouting to the youth of America. Copies of Baden Powell's book "Scouting for Boys", had reached the United States even before the incorporation of the Boy Scouts of America. Men interested in boys had made the first attempts to help establish Boy Scout troops. Among these men was <u>Edgar M. Robinson</u> of the National Organization of the Young Men's Christian Association (Y.M.C.A.).

As Secretary of the Committee on Boy's Work, Robinson followed the growing interest in Scouting among boys throughout the country. He received many letters asking about the Boy Scout program.

The Y.M.C.A. was not in a position to take on Scouting on a national basis, but it was able to help boys locally get the benefit of the Scout program. By 1909, Robinson informed local Y.M.C.A.'s how they may be of assistance.

Robinson became concerned because several Scout associations sprung up and began competing against one another. Among them were: <u>"Boy Scouts of United States"</u>, <u>"National Scouts of America"</u>, <u>"Peace Scouts of California"</u>, and <u>"American Boy Scout"</u>. Some of these groups were of military or otherwise undesirable character.

Robinson was determined to have the Boy Scout movement in America united and dedicated to the original ideals and program of Scouting that Baden Powell created. When Robinson learned that a group named "Boy Scouts of America" was incorporated, he decided that this legally established corporation might be the nucleus of the single organization that he invisioned.

With a couple of Y.M.C.A. colleagues, Robinson went to Chicago to see Boyce to persuade him of the idea of one national organization and to offer the cooperation of the Y.M.C.A. in getting the organization under way. Boyce consented.

On June 21, 1910, in the Board Room of the International Committee of the Y.M.C.A. at 124 East 28th Street in New York, a group of men of national reputation and with experience and interest in work for boys gathered to determine what steps might be taken to create the movement that Robinson was strongly for.

These men represented thirty-seven different organizations concerned with boys: Y.M.C.A., Y.M.H.A., Playground Association, Big Brother Movement, Public School Athletic League, existing Boy Scout groups, boy organizations such as the "Woodcraft Indians", the "Sons of Daniel Boone", and others, as well as business men, educators, authors, editors and publishers.

These men decided to proceed with the creation of a permanent organization, national in scope, and a committee to nominate the men who should head it. Ernest Thompson Seton, head of the organization called "Woodcraft Indians" became chairman of the Committee-On-Organization. John L. Alexander of the Philadelphia Y.M.C.A. was made managing Secretary to handle the increasing volume of requests for information.

The Committee on Organization brought into the new movement other existing boys' groups and the other Boy Scout organizations. The "American Boy Scout" organization refused to cooperate and later dissolved following court action. The committee also formulated a set of bylaws, and convinced many men of national reputation to associate themselves with the movement as members of a National Council. Even the president of the United States at that time, William Howard Taft, was made Honorary President, and Theodore Roosevelt as Honorary Vice President and Chief Scout Citizen.

On October 25, 1910, the original incorporation met and elected a Board of Managers (later renamed Executive Board), and on October 27, 1910, the Committee on Organization, now finished with its work, handed over to this board its records and holdings. Colin H. Livingstone was elected President and Ernest Thompson Seton, Chief Scout. The first three National Scout Commissioners assigned were: Daniel Carter Beard, head of the "Sons of Daniel Boone"; Adjutant-General William Verbeck, formerly of the "National Scouts of America"; and Colonel Peter S. Bomus, of the "Boy Scouts of the United States".

The Boy Scouts of America was now established as a functioning, independent organization, dedicated to the welfare of the American boy.

To direct the Boy Scouts of America, the Executive Board chose a young Washington attorney by the name of James Edward West.

Three men were to have a tremendous influence on the early development of the new movement: West, Seton, and Beard.

West was an administrator, Seton and Beard were outdoorsmen, artists, and authors like Baden Powell. Ernest Thompson Seton and Daniel Carter Beard directed rival youth organizations. Seton headed the "Woodcraft Indians", and Beard headed the "Sons of Daniel Boone".

Ernest Thompson Seton was a tall man with a lot of unruly hair and a bushy mustache. He was born in England in 1860 but immigrated to Canada at an early age. The wilderness of the American continent excited him to such an extent that he decided to become a naturalist. While working as a Canadian artist and naturalist for the provincial government in Manitoba he picked up another interest: a desire to help perpetuate the lore of the American Indian.

Coming to the United States, Seton combined his knowledge of nature with his writing and illustrating abilities to create a number of highly successful books. Among his writings were: "Wild Animals I Have Known", "The Biography of a Grizzly", "Lives of the Hunted", and "Two Little Savages".

His Indian interests led him to establish a youth organization which he called the "Woodcraft Indians". Their code was based on Indian Tribal laws and a program of Indian games, skills and rituals. The purpose of the organization was "to give the young people something to do, something to think about, and something to enjoy in the woods, with view always to character build, for manhood, not scholarship, is the first aim of education".

His rich background of woodcraft, camping and other outdoor skills made Seton a logical choice for a Chief Scout of the Boy Scouts of America. He remained Chief Scout for five years.

Daniel Carter Beard was affectionately known by all Boy Scouts as "Uncle Dan". He was a man of medium height, with a clipped mustache and neatly trimmed goatee.

He was born in Ohio in 1850, but soon after moved to Kentucky were the territory was rich with the legends of Daniel Boone.

Dan Beard had his mind set on an art career, and after the Civil War he arrived in New York to study at the Art Students' League. His magazine and book illustrations became so popular that he was chosen to illustrate Mark Twain's "A Connecticut Yankee in King Arthur's Court".

Beard had brought with him to New York the recollections of lively boyhood spent in woods and fields, and a love for the skills and the spirit of the pioneers who had opened up the western frontiers. He shared this heritage with all American boys through articles and drawings in the pages of "St. Nicholas Magazine", and "Youth's Companion". These articles were later published in book form in the popular "American Boys' Handy Book", and "Outdoor Handy Book". Beard also wrote and illustrated the "Buckskin Book for Buckskin Men and Boys".

As a further step to keep alive the traditions and activities of the "American Knights in Buckskin" and "to educate our lads early in life to an appreciation of the absolute necessity and value of our forests and natural resources" he formed "The Society of the Sons of Daniel Boone."

When the Boy Scouts of America came into being, Dan Beard joined it enthusiastically as National Commissioner and Chairman of the National Court of Honor, and wrote and illustrated articles for the Boy Scout magazine, BOY'S LIFE, until his death in 1941, ten days before his 91st birthday.

James E. West was born in 1876 in Washington D.C. His early years were full of tradedy. His father died before Jimmy was born. When he was six, his mother was forced to put him in an orphan home while she went to the hospital. Within a year she was dead of tuberculosis, leaving Jimmy without any known relatives.

Jimmy was a healthy boy. But shortly after being in the orphan home he began to limp and complain of pains in one hip. The people in charge of the orphanage thought the boy was faking to get out of work. He was whipped. His leg did not improve.

Finally he was sent to a hospital where the doctors diagnosed a tubercular hip. Jimmy was kept in the hospital for nearly two years. Much of that time he was strapped to a board with weights on his leg. He was then pronounced an incurable cripple and sent back to the orphanage. He was now so lame that he could not do the work the boys were supposed to do. He was given the bitter task of sewing and mending with the orphan girls.

When he was twelve, an old friend of his mother came to see him. She was Mrs. Ellis Spear, wife of the United States Patent Commissioner, and a writer of children's books. She gave Jimmy one of her books and invited him to visit her home. For the first time in his life Jimmy was taken into a family circle with five vigorous children. Mrs. Spear aroused his interest in reading and spurred his determination to secure an education. At the age of sixteen, Jimmy asked the matron of the orphanage for permission to go to high school. This was unheard of for orphan children in the 1890's. After some persuasion he was given his wish as long as he did not let his work in the orphanage suffer.

Jimmy was well liked by his school friends. He became editor of the school paper and, in spite of his crutches, business manager of the school's football team.

By the time Jimmy West graduated high school, he had made up his mind to become a lawyer. He got the chance to go to law school and to read law with an attorney. To support himself he secured work at the Washington Y.M.C.A. and as a government stenographer.

After graduating from law school at age 25, young West was appointed to the Board of Pension Appeals and later was made assistant attorney in the Department of the Interior. At last he could afford good clothes and a decent place to live.

West approached the President of the United States, Theodore Roosevelt, and persuaded him to call a conference on child care. West served as secretary of the conference and was mainly responsible for its success. Out of this first White House Conference on the Care of Dependent Children, organized by West, eventually came the Children's Bureau of the Department of Labor.

West was involved with other work for youth. He dedicated himself to help all children, healthy, sick or handicapped, to have a better life. His work made him aware of further needs of children. Now age 34, it was this experienced youth worker who was asked by the Executive Board of the newly formed Boy Scouts of America to head the movement. And on January 2, 1911, James E. West opened a National Scout Office in the Fifth Avenue Building, 200 Fifth Avenue, New York, and went to work.

West led the Boy Scouts of America for 32 years. He was a strong and wise leader. He helped build Scouting into the largest boy movement in the country and in the free world.

The first OFFICIAL HANDBOOK of the Boy Scouts of America was published hurriedly in 1910. It was an Americanized version of Baden Powell's "Scouting For Boys". In it, the boys of America could read about joining a Scout Patrol, about fun in the outdoors, about hiking and camping. There were games to play and badges to earn. It also contained the Scout Oath and Law adapted from the English Oath and Law. Immediately, boys by the thousands became Scouts.

Since the start of the Scout movement in America, February 8, 1910, over 30 million copies of Boy Scout handbooks in nine editions have been sold.

BOY'S LIFE MAGAZINE was started by Joseph Lane at age 18 in Providence, Rhode Island. It was an ideal title for a magazine for boys.

The Boy Scouts of America decided to buy the magazine from Lane. Subscriptions at that time numbered 6,100.

From 6,100 in 1912, Boys Life Magazine grew to be a national magazine with more than 6,000,000 subscribers.

Norman Rockwell, the best known and most beloved American artist at age 18 in 1912, joined Boys Life Magazine as illustrator and art director. During his career, he painted more than 500 paintings. His success was based on his skill and his high standards. Once he wrote in gold paint on the top of his easel, "100%". A friend asked him, "What does that mean?" he answered, "That's what Norman expects of Norman".

BOY SCOUT SERVICE was given in times of flood, fire, hurricane and other disasters, as well as helping at parades and at civic gatherings during the years that followed. They justified their motto, "BE PREPARED".

Congress granted a Federal Charter to the Boy Scouts of America on June 15, 1916, because they had proved themselves such useful citizens. The charter protected the name and insignia, and authorized the Scout uniform so that no one but Scouts might use the uniform of Scouting.

When the First World War came, Scouts rushed to help their country. They sold Liberty Bonds and Stamps totalling $406,859,262, they located 20,758,660 feet of Walnut for airplanes, they collected 100 carloads of fruit pits needed for gas masks, they conducted war gardens, they distributed 30,000,000 pieces of Government literature, besides helping the Red Cross and many other organizations.

In the Second World War, Scouts lived up to their traditions. They helped Civilian Defense as messengers, they served as forewatchers and aids to emergency medical units, they raised Victory Gardens, they salvaged waste paper and collected scrap metal, they served as official dispatch bearers for important government messages, and they organized Emergency Service Corps to aid the community.

The FIRST WORLD JAMBOREE was held in 1920. By then Scouting had spread around the world. Baden Powell saw the Scout movement becoming an international brotherhood. To strengthen this world brotherhood, Baden Powell called Scouts from all nations where the movement had taken hold to a World Jamboree in London, England where 301 Scouts attended from 32 countries. During this first world gathering of Scouts, Baden Powell was acclaimed "Chief Scout Of The World".

The jamboree was a great success. It showed the people of the world what Scouting was, and what Scouts could do. More and more countries took up Scouting.

The day the movement reached its 21st birthday, Scouting was found in practically every civilized country. On that occassion Baden Powell was honored by his King, George V, by being created a Baron under the name of <u>Lord Baden Powell Of Gilwell</u>.

Since the First World Jamboree in 1920, world jamborees have been held every 4 years, with the exception of the World War II years.

The Boy Scouts of America took up the idea on a national basis. In 1937, the <u>First National Jamboree</u> was held in Washington, D.C. with 27,232 Scouts and leaders who camped at the foot of the Washington Monument. National Jamborees have been held between World Jamborees since then with as many as 50,000 Scouts taking part.

The Boy Scouts of America continued to grow. More and more Boy Scouts joined in those early years.

<u>Sea Scouting</u> was established in 1912 in the Boy Scouts of America to hold older boys. Then it became <u>Senior Scouting</u> and showed a spurt in membership. In 1919, it was turned into <u>Exploring</u> which is now the program for young men and women in the Boy Scouts of America.

In 1924, the <u>Lone Scouts of America</u> merged with the Boy Scouts of America. The Lone Scouts of America was organized by William D. Boyce, who brought Scouting to the United States.

<u>Cub Scouting</u>, a younger boy program in the Boy Scouts of America, started in 1930. It was originally called "Cubbing". It began to draw boys from 8 years of age and up into the movement.

Today the Boy Scouts of America is the largest youth movement in the free world, with over 14 million members in more than 100 countries.

SCOUTING COMES TO YOUNGSTOWN

In 1911, just one year after the Boy Scout program came to America, a group of very interested Youngstown Community Leaders brought Scouting to Youngstown.

In 1912, the first three troops were organized in the council. They were Troop 9 sponsored by the First Presbyterian Church in Girard with Minister Jesse H. Beard serving as Scoutmaster, Troop 19 sponsored by the Rodef Sholem Temple with Herbert Hartzell serving as Scoutmaster, and Troop 23 sponsored by Richard Brown Memorial Church with R.C. McBride serving as Scoutmaster. In 1918, Troop 23 reorganized as Troop 4.

In 1913, the first local council charters were issued by the Boy Scouts of America. Youngstown leaders responded quickly and on March 25, 1913, the first organizational meeting to discuss chartering took place in the directors room of the First National Bank in downtown Youngstown. George W. Alloway, Haselton School Principle, presided. Reverend James Baird, assistant pastor of the First Presbyterian Church acted as secretary. Mr. Horton of Pittsburgh and Father Kirby of the Girard Catholic Church spoke on the Scout program.

The council was organized at another session the following week. John H. Chase of the Playground Association served as chairman until officers were named. During this meeting a nominating committee was appointed consisting of Dr. C.O. Brown, Phillip J. Thompson, and Lionel Evans. At their suggestion the following officers were elected: George L. Fordyce as Council President (Fordyce was owner of the Fordyce Company which was located at the corner of West Federal and South Phelps streets); J.P. Colleran as Vice-President (Colleran was president of City Council); Henry A. Butler as Secretary (Butler was owner of Wick and Company); and James L. Wick Jr. as Treasurer (Wick was owner of Falcon Bronze Company). A committee of A.H. Dillon, W.W. Zimmerman, and R. R.E. Whelan was appointed to draw up a constitution and bylaws which were later adopted. P.J. Thompson, Dr. George Peck, Leo Guthman, Hugh Grant and Lionel Evans were named to nominate a Scout Commissioner. John H. Chase, who also served temporarily as volunteer Council Executive, was secured for Scout Commissioner.

Shortly after this, Grant, Dr. C.O. Brown, and J. Pearnley Bonnell were added to the list of officers as members of the Executive Committee. P.J. Thompson became chairman of the Court of Honor. Other active workers at that time were Herbert S. Hartzell, I. Harry Meyer, Harry Levinson, R.C. McBride, and Phil Hardy. Then P.L. Fratley became volunteer Council Executive.

The Boy Scout program in Youngstown
was granted charter for the first time on
April 1, 1913 as "Youngstown Council".

The "Youngstown Council" had supervision over Youngstown, Girard, and Niles. In 1914 there were over 300 boys enrolled in our council and our first council summer camp was created and named "Camp Thompson".

During the first five years every effort was made to carry on the program through volunteer and community leaders who were employed elsewhere for such programs as playgrounds.

In 1927, the name "Youngstown Council" was changed to "Mahoning Valley Council". The council had supervision over all of Mahoning County, Hubbard Township in Trumbull County, and Deerfield and Palmyra Townships in Portage County. Until 1927, there were no definite boundaries. By the end of 1927 we had 51 troops with 1144 Scouts.

As the years passed, councils throughout the country found it difficult to operate independently. Small councils began merging with larger councils or consolidating with other small councils.

On February 10, 1993, Mahoning Valley Council, Northeast Ohio Council in Painesville, and Western Reserve Council in Warren voted to consolidate into one new council under a new name, thus ending the story of Mahoning Valley Council.

This book does not include every person or event that existed during the past 82 years of Mahoning Valley Council. This book is intended to highlight some of the main events and to mention some of the people involved.

Youngstown Scouts, circa 1917-1927. Behind them is the basement window to the one room council office that faced Rayen Avenue in the Reuben-McMillan Library. Worn out words on the window read: "Boy Scouts of America".

BOY SCOUTS IN MAHONING COUNTY

AH-CHAY-TEE. Ah-Chay-Tee means, "Friendly Little Fire". It was a ceremony performed around a campfire each week of summer camp in the area of the now known Elm Campsite. This ceremony emphasized making new friends in camp, and it told the story of camp. Council Executive Henry Katschke started Ah-Chay-Tee when he came to Youngstown in 1949. It phased out around 1968 when Katschke retired. Part of the ceremony included Scouts picking up a rock from the creek they crossed as they left the fire. The rock was placed on a pile of rocks in the Spruce Triangle which represented the many Scouts who had come to camp in previous years.

ALPHA PHI OMEGA. There was an active chapter of the Alpha Phi Omega fraternity at Youngstown State University in 1968. The staff advisor was District Executive Don Bordenaro.

A fine relationship existed between the University and the Boy Scouts of America. The chapter office was in Kilcawley Hall where they held their meetings on Monday nights.

AMERICAN YOUTH AWARD. In early 1926, Eagle Scout William Campbell of Troop 12 was nominated for and received the American Youth Award. One boy and one girl were selected from each state to be entered at the Sesqui Centennial Exposition held at Philadelphia. Scout Campbell had first gained distinction when he saved a small child from death beneath the wheels of a train. The girl receiving the American Youth Award was Miss Dorothy Luzler who served as office secretary at Scout headquarters in the early 30's.

ANNIVERSARIES. By the 29th National Anniversary in 1939, the Boy Scouts of America membership numbered 1,271,900. The highlight of the celebration was an address at the White House by President Roosevelt that was broadcast at 10:00 pm over the nation's networks. An article in the Vindicator read: "...People in general, along with President Roosevelt, like to think of the entire Scout training as an apprenticeship for mastery of civic duties."

ANNUAL DINNER MEETING. A special council wide dinner meeting is held every year to recognize Scouts and leaders for their achievements. The first Annual Dinner Meeting was held in 1913.

At the 1918, two representatives of the National Staff, Lorne W. Barclay and James A. Wilder, were guests of honor and speakers. Mr. Wilder originated the "Sea Scout" program in 1912 for older boys and was Chief Sea Scout. He talked about the Sea Scout program being changed in 1919 to the "Exploring" program. The election of council officers resulted in the installation of James L. Wick Jr. as Council President, and E.S. Brown as Scout Commissioner.

At the 1919 meeting held at the close of the year, E.S. Brown was elected president of the council with E. Mason Wick as commissioner. The outstanding event of the administration was the erection of the camp mess hall at the Stambaugh Scout Reservation. The building which had been a sheep barn at the top of the hill near Leffingwell Road was moved down the hill on skids using a Model-T Ford. This was done with the assistance of neighboring farmers and others.

Years end at the 1924 meeting, Myron C. Wick Jr. became Council President, W.S. Hogg continued as Commissioner.

In 1944 and 1945, the meeting was held at the Y.M.C.A.

In 1952, the 39th Annual Council Meeting was held at the Y.M.C.A. Attorney Robert A. Manchester was re-elected to his fourth term as Council President.

It was reported that 27 Scouts were awarded Eagles in 1951, and that 4,027 youths were active in Mahoning Valley Council.

At the March 1958 meeting, Dr. Pliny H. Powers, superintendent of Youngstown schools from 1937 to 1941 and deputy Scout executive of the National Council of the Boy Scouts of America in 1958, was principal speaker at the dinner in Stambaugh Auditorium. More than 400 were in attendance.

Dr. Powers traced the history of Scouting in the Mahoning Valley since its beginning. He outlined the technological and social changes that have occurred in that time, and said "the effects of these changes on today's youth make the Scouting program more important than ever". That was in 1958!

He continued saying, "Society cannot guarantee every boy a devoted and intelligent mother and a wise and provident father, but society can guarantee every child a competent and well trained teacher, a good Scout leader and a devoted Sunday school teacher."

Commenting on recent publicity regarding juvenile delinquency, he said, "The first thing to remember is that a boy who is loved, wanted, trusted and given regular duties from his earliest years is not likely to become delinquent."

The "President's Award" was given to Pioneer District for best all over participation in the Scouting program. This award was established the year before in 1957 by outgoing president G. Taylor Evans.

Each Scouting unit that contributed the previous year to the Council's World Friendship fund for rehabilitating the Scouting program in war torn countries was awarded a special citation. Mahoning Valley Council raised $287 for the fund in 1957.

Boy Scout Ronald Keslar of Troop 32 in Ellsworth accepted a citation from Dr. Powers on behalf of his unit. Other units also received a citation. A symbol of this world wide program was a globe with a Scout hat on top.

At the 56th meeting in 1969, a new constitution and regulations for the Mahoning Valley Council were approved. The new constitution and regulations made provisions for the establishment of an Advisory Council to the Council Executive Board composed of men who have either retired or have reached the age of 70 years.

ARTESIAN SULFUR WELL. In the 1920's, Harry Walker made a drinking fountain out of an artesian sulfur well that was located along the creek just below the dam. Scouts from yesteryear recall the sulfur odor to be quite bad. It was washed away during the 1956 flood.

ASSEMBLY FIELD. Sometimes referred to as parade field, it was an open flat area where the camp would meet for flag ceremonies and camp-wide events. Three well known assembly field sites were used in Camp Stambaugh. One was less than 200 feet from Leffingwell Road between Beech Knob and Aspen Campsites. A remnant of a flat cement base with a cut off steel stub of a flag pole still lay hidden on the ground. An inscribed date in the cement reads 1941.

Another assembly site still used today is in the Walker area in front of the Walker Cabin. District events and training courses were usually based in this area.

The main assembly field used in camp from the beginning in 1919 is the flat area at the bottom of the hill by the creek near the dining hall. Tens of thousands of Scouts, leaders, parents and guests have watched flag ceremonies since 1919 to the sound of one or more bugles and during some years, the firing of a miniature canon.

The first flag pole used on the main assembly field was a 60 foot tall wood pole twelve inches wide at the base set in concrete. Then sometime in 1930 or 1940, a four section 50 foot tall steel pole replaced the wood pole. The steel pole was later placed on the Herbert Hartzell Memorial Flagpole Platform that was built and dedicated August 1967. The platform was constructed 45 feet behind the original flag pole site. It was donated by Mrs. Frances Schwebel Greenberger and dedicated to the memory of Herbert Hartzell who was a Silver Beaver and Scoutmaster of Rodef Sholom Temple, Troop 19.

In the fall of 1972, an Army reserve work party welded a pivot at the base of the pole in order to lower it making repairs to the pulley easier.

(1) Looking over a 1931 copy of the Vindicator during the 1958 Recognition Dinner is (left to right): Council Executive Henry Katschke, National Council Deputy Chief Executive Dr. Pliny Powers, Council President James Beeghly, and Regional Scout Executive W.B. Hubbell. (2) Archery Range, 1950. (photo by Henry Katschke). (3) February 1922 Anniversary exhibit. Troop 17 with Scoutmaster Harry Walker camped at Central Square in downtown Youngstown. The Dollar Savings and Trust Company building is at left. (4) Assembly Field, June, 1919. (5) Note wood flag pole on Assembly Field, 1919. Conrad Meinecke is pictured at front left. (6) Herbert Hartzell Memorial Flagpole Platform, 1967. (photo by Lee Banks).

BADEN POWELL CABIN. The Baden Powell cabin was built in 1930 by one of the council's first troops, Troop 9 from the First Presbyterian Church of Girard.

The Cabin was named in honor of Baden Powell, the founder of Scouting.

The cabin has been used during the summer camp season as a nature lodge and handicraft cabin. During the other seasons it was rented for use by Scout units on week-ends.

BADEN POWELL VISITS DETROIT MICHIGAN. Baden Powell made a tour of the United States in 1926. He did not come to Youngstown, but a group of Scouts and leaders made the trip to Detroit where Baden Powell visited.

Three Youngstown boys had the thrill of having their Eagle Scout badges pinned on their chests by Baden Powell.

BAIRD, FREDERICK L. Council Executive for Mahoning Valley Council from 1985-1993. (also see Section IV).

Fred first started working with Scouting while attending Anderson College. He was on the Explorer committee, then later accepted advisor position for the general interest post. After moving to Michigan, he remained active on the Cub committee in Charlotte, Michigan. From 1960-1970, Fred was in the ministry, 3 years in Michigan and 7 years at the New Springfield Church of God.

While a minister in New Springfield, he started Pack, Troop, and Post #119 serving as Institutional Representative for 7 years.

In a 1976 interview, when asked what his best enjoyment in Scouting was, he answered, "Working with the many people from all walks of life and having the responsibility of servicing scouts and leaders and seeing the Scout program work successfully. But the uttermost enjoyment is, knowing that I have been part of a very important youth program in the world."

Fred's hobby has always been woodworking. He built his own home and separate workshop on his New Springfield property. His home displays his fine craftsmanship in the cabinets, furniture and rooms he has built. He has a collection of wood toys that he designed and made.

BALABAN, MIKE. Mike was an active Scouter for over 34 years until his death in 1984. He served every position in Scouting on the district and council level. He was awarded his Woodbadge and Silver Beaver.

The most memorable times I remember with Mike is while he was training chairman for the council. He asked me, first at age 16, to participate on the training staff as bugler and to teach camping skills. From then on, I served on just about all of his training courses and when I began to run training courses, Mike served on my staff.

As the years went on, every spring I would take Mike with me to Big Oaks in Highlandtown so I could learn about eatable plants. Mike was a very good naturalist. After our day in the woods, I would take Mike to a steak house like Bonanza or Ponderosa for a steak dinner. He would always dazzle the other patrons when while at the dinner table he pulled out that plastic bag he always carried around and a pocket knife. In the plastic bag were wild onions from the woods. He diced them over our steaks while others just looked on!

BEARD, DANIEL CARTER. Daniel Carter Beard was one of the two originators of the Boy Scout movement. He visited Youngstown Council in 1919 as a guest speaker for the 9th Annual Anniversary meeting.

Dan Beard was the National Commissioner until his death at age 91. He was awarded the only solid gold Eagle Scout badge. All of his awards can be seen in the museum at Bear Mountain State Park in New York.

BEARD, JESSE H. Jesse Beard was Scoutmaster of Troop 9 from 1912-1913. Then he entered the seminary to become a minister.

Some of his troop members included: Sidney Jackson, Edgar Leedy Jr., and Steve Bromley.

BENCH MARKS. Two known bench marks in Camp Stambaugh are: (1) at the entrance into camp where the elevation is 1132 feet and (2) at the assembly field on the Hartzell Memorial Flagpole Platform where the elevation is 1030.6 feet.

BIG OAK WILDERNESS CAMP. In April of 1963, 422 acres of beautiful rolling land in southern Columbiana County was a gift from Mr. & Mrs. Arnold Stambaugh. The Stambaugh's purchased the land for $13,000. Arnold was a Council Executive Board member and owner and president of Stambaugh Hardwood Lumber Company. He was not related to Henry Stambaugh who gave the property for Camp Stambaugh.

The camp was near Highlandtown on Route 39, seven miles west of Wellsville. It had a large number of huge oak trees and an old run down farm house beyond repair that was torn down later. The date on the stone fireplace inside the cellar of the house read, "18--". The last two figures were chipped off.

The front section of the property was bare due to previous farming. Reforestation plans developed by the State Conservation Service included planting thousands of trees in the years to follow.

In 1967, the camping committee sponsored a contest to name the property. One name only was allowed to be submitted by each unit. The reason why the name was selected by the unit was to accompany the submission.

Only 14 units responded each with a different name and reason. Since the camp had many large oak trees on it, the name "Big Oak" was selected from the list.

In the spring of 1968, 10,000 seedlings which included the red, white pitch, Virginia, and short-leafed pine, were planted on 75 acres of the property. Other planting projects took place for several years under plans developed by the State Conservation Service.

In 1969, the Engineering Service of the National Boy Scout Headquarters visited Camp Big Oak. They reviewed the property with Director of Council Camping, Bart Ingram and Camp Committee member, Bob Lacelle to decide on the feasibility of development for a permanent camp. Campsites and two lakes of about 6-8 acres each were discussed. The only camp improvement ever made however, was fixing the only hand operated water pump on the property and constructing a pole building shell that was donated by Clarence Smith. Lack of money stopped further progress of development.

On July 11, 1971, our council operated a primitive summer camp in Big Oak. It only operated one year due to lack of funding.

Bart Ingram of our professional staff created and developed the summer camp program. Tony Valley Jr. was camp Director. Staff members included Nick Valley, Jerry Evanoff, Ken Goist and Scott Callahan.

The wilderness camp ran for four weeks and incorporated four outpost camps. The program involved nature study, wilderness survival living, rifle and skeet shooting, hunting, astronomy, map and compass, and cooking. Scouts attending Camp Big Oak backpacked to two outpost camps and rode mini-trail bikes to the other outpost camps.

In 1974, the pole building was moved to Camp Stambaugh due to vandalism.

Since 1963, Camp Big Oak was used for camporees, troop camping and Philmont training, until it was sold for strip mining around 1981.

BOYPOWER '76. On January 1, 1969, the Mahoning Valley Council launched an eight year long program called BOYPOWER '76. The slogan for this ambitious eight year program was "America's MANPOWER begins with BOYPOWER."

This program created by national was to broaden membership base and make known to boys, leaders and local organizations the availability of the Scouting program to all who can accept its commitment of service to god, country and other people.

BRAMMER BOULEVARD. Some time during the early 1970s, the road into camp that went down the hill was fixed and paved. Jack Brammer, an active Scouter on the Camping Committee, and his company donated the equipment and material for this project. A road sign named "Brammer Boulevard" was erected on a pole near the road at the top of the hill.

BRIDGES IN CAMP STAMBAUGH. The bridge that crosses Indian Creek just below the dam was built in 1925 by Troop 8. Prior to that time, a wood foot bridge was used.

In 1952, sixty Explorer Scouts received instruction from Marine Corps engineers on methods of bridge construction. The boys, ages 14 through 17, spent the entire day receiving instruction from 9 marine instructors headed by Captain George Babe, Third Engineer Company, Marine Corps Reserve.

Half of the Scout group constructed a floating foot bridge across Indian Lake from the dock west of the island below the Roosevelt cabin. A second group used numerous power tools in construction of a 42 foot timber trestle bridge that crossed the ravine from White Oak campsite to Black Oak campsite.

BROWN, KENNETH L. In May of 1936, Kenneth L. Brown came to Youngstown to be Council Executive from Wheeling, West Virginia where he was Council Executive.

On May 16th, 1949 at the Y.M.C.A., a group of 80 Scout leaders and their wives honored Kenneth L. Brown and Mrs. Brown at a farewell retirement dinner. Brown retired because of ill health and later moved to Florida.

BROWN, M.E. M.E. Brown, Jr., former Boy Scout Camp Director for Logan and Huntington, West Virginia, became Director of Camping for the Mahoning Valley Boy Scout Council, and District Scout Executive of the Pioneer District on October 15, 1951. He served as camp director in 1951.

Brown replaced Robert Kling, who was the former ranger at the Scout Reservation. Kling resigned September 1, 1951 to take a position with the Smith Dairy.

Brown and his wife lived in the home at the Scout Reservation.

BROWN PAVILION. The K.L. Brown Pavilion was built in 1947 and named after our third Council Executive who served from 1936 to 1949.

The pavilion was built of logs with a cement floor. It replaced the Stambaugh farm's old hay barn. The foundation under the pavilion is the same foundation that supported the barn.

Prior to 1919, the red barn housed some of the farm animals, hay and farm harvests. When the farm became the Stambaugh Scout Reservation in 1919, only one horse named "Barney" remained on the property. Barney stayed in the lower portion of the barn with an entrance from the rear of the foundation.

The barn was used on the Stambaugh Scout Reservation until 1947 when it was replaced by the pavilion. A camp workshop and garage was added and in 1965 a modern

toilet facility was also added under the pavilion with entrance in the back.

Before comfortable mattresses were used in camp, Scouts filled their mattress sacks with straw from the red barn to sleep on. Before the 1950s, Indian Creek at the bottom of the hill by the flag pole could be seen from the pavilion. The land in between was still open field.

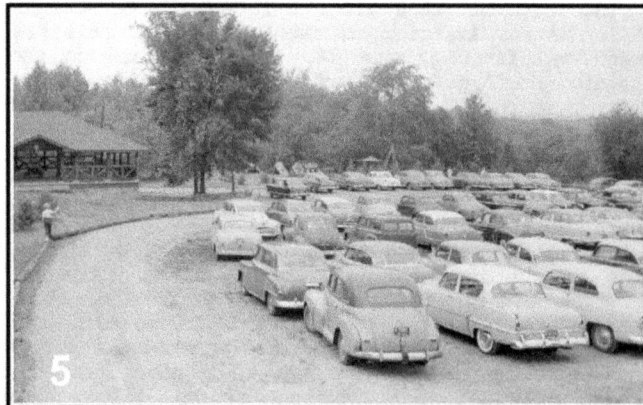

(1) Daniel . Carter Beard (1931) was National Commissioner until his death at age 91. (2) Council President James L. Beeghly (1957-1959). (3) J.C. Brownlee, 1966. (photo by Lee Banks). (4) Kenneth L. Brown, 1949. (5) K.L. Brown Pavilion and parking lot, 1954. (photo by Lee Banks).

CAMP COMMITTEE. The first Camp Committee for the Stambaugh Scout Reservation was formed in 1919. The chairman was Lloyd R. Wallis. Some of the committee members were W.W. Zimmerman, E.S. Brown, Harry A. Boyd, and Paul McElevey.

The camp committee was responsible for the development and maintenance of the Stambaugh Scout Reservation facilities and program.

In the mid 1970s, the committee was divided into two committees. The Camp Committee, now responsible for program, and the Properties Committee, responsible for maintenance.

CAMP COMMITTEE CHAIRMEN	
1919	Lloyd R. Wallis
*	Sidney S. Moyer
1950-1951	Walter Chuck
*	M.M. Malmer
*	John Schaefer
*	Wayne Stoyer
1967-1968	Leo Poulakis
1968-1972	Fred Bailey
*	Dick Robart
1989-1993	Jack Bokesch

CAMP DIRECTORS. The following have served as Camp Director for the Summer Camp program at Stambaugh Scout Reservation, unless otherwise noted, since its beginning in 1919.

CAMP DIRECTORS	
1914-1917	Phillip J. Thompson (see "Camp Thompson")
1918	K.F. Miller (see "Camp Hitchcock")
1919-1921	K.F. Miller
1922-1945	Harry A. Walker
*	
1949	J.B. Austin
1950	Hyer Martin
1951-1952	M.E. Brown
*	
1954	Harry Clover
*	
1956-1966	Lou Flickinger
1967-1971	Bart Ingram
1972	Bill Hill
1973	Jim Wilhide/Jack LeBrun
1974	Jack LeBrun/Tony Valley Jr.
1975-1976	Paul Luke
1977-1978	Bob Hands
1979-1981	Jeff Dyer
1982-1983	Dom Lucarell
1984	Jeff Dyer
1985	Jack LeBrun
1986	Jeff Dyer
1987-1988	Don Ruse
1989	Glen Duncan
1990-1991	Tony Valley Jr.
1992	John Palo

CAMP IMPROVEMENT, 1919-1968. From the very beginning, Scouts, Scouters, and friends of Scouting have worked long and hard to maintain and improve Camp Stambaugh. The following are a few highlights of some major camp improvement projects done at Camp Stambaugh.

1919- The Stambaugh Reservation was open fields. The creek at the bottom of the farm could be seen from the old barn where the K.L. Brown Pavilion now stands. Only fruit orchards and meadows existed.

The first conservation project to plant trees on the reservation began. Mr. Meyer from Ritter and Meyer along with his wife, Helen Strouss Meyer, financed the reforesting of the Stambaugh Scout Reservation.

A small mud hole was dug along Indian Creek for a swimming pool.

A small cabin was built on the north shore of Indian Creek called "Chief's Cabin". It was made of logs cut in camp.

In the fall, the sheep barn on the farm was moved to the bottom of camp using skids and a Model-T so it could become the camp dining hall.

1922- A plan was under way to build a permanent dam, install the necessary sanitation as advised by the State Board of Health, and improve a road on one of the hills in camp at a total cost of $5,000. The improvements had the endorsement of the Community Chest Corporation and the active backing of 200 men who were interested in Boy Scout work.

Two troop shelters were erected, one by a troop with Scoutmaster H.H. Smith. The other shelter was built in the spring near the swimming hole by Troop 4 with C.R. Betts as Scoutmaster.

1923- In the spring, several improvements were installed at the camp following a special campaign for funds. The principal improvement was the construction of a four acre lake.

1946- The Stambaugh Scout Reservation at this time was considered the heart of Scout activities.

The Capital Fund Campaign of 1946 began in April. Campaign chairman Dr. Russell J. Humbert announced a drive to raise $100,000 for expansion and rebuilding of Stambaugh Scout Reservation to make possible for the highest type of camping experience for boys of the community.

1947- This years camp improvement projects resulted from the 1946 Capital Fund Campaign.

The first hard surface road was laid down as a service road on the reservation and the parking lot was constructed. Basic electrical power lines were installed. The Walker Cabin was built from a natural log kit in honor of Camp Ranger Harry A. Walker. The Strouss Cabin was also built from a log kit identical to the Walker Cabin. It was built in memory of Executive Board Member Isaac Strouss. A log cabin was built from a kit to replace the farm house that burned down in 1945. This became the Camp Ranger's home. The K.L. Brown pavilion replaced the Stambaugh Farm's red hay barn on the same foundation. The pavilion was constructed of logs with a concrete floor. Under the pavilion with entrance on the back side, was the camp workshop and garage. The pavilion was named in honor of the Council Executive Kenneth L. Brown.

1949- A group of Youngstown business men and Scout enthusiasts recognized the need for continued improvement at the reservation and began a movement to build up the camp. Work parties began. Scout leaders and friends from the county voluntarily spent their Saturdays at the camp helping in the project. But money and lumber were needed. The Heller-Murray Company, informed of the camp's problem, presented it to the Lumberman Dealer's Association. Soon after, lumber began arriving at the camp free of charge. Word of the camp's condition spread throughout the area. Contributions from various sources began to arrive. The Rotary Club built bleachers around the camp's Council Fire Ring. The Lions Club donated an electric dishwasher. Carlson Electric rewired Meinecke Lodge which was the main building in camp, and Arnold Stambaugh paid for other repairs on the same lodge. Standard Slag Company contributed by sending out huge trucks filled with enough slag to cover all the roads. These and other gifts made Camp Stambaugh a more livable and healthful place for Boy Scouts to camp.

Other organizations that helped in camp maintenance are: Boardman Lions Club, Mill Creek Kiwanis, and C.B. Units. At a Council Fire ceremony Thursday evening, August 9th, 1951, a silver plaque commemorating the 58 individuals and companies who contributed to the improvement of Camp Stambaugh was presented to the camp by Camping Committee Chairman Walter Chuck. Replicas of the plaque were sent to the 58 individuals and firms. More than 800 attended the presentation which ended the final week of summer camp that year.

1955- Eight years after the hard service road into camp was constructed, repairs had to be made.

Five welded tubular constructed wash stands were donated at a cost of $300 each and placed at strategic locations around the camp. The water was gravity fed from holding tanks on top of the stand. These tanks were drained during the winter season to prevent freezing. The water jets at the basin always got clogged over winter from rust. The wash stands were installed in concrete with wooden platforms for Scouts to stand on. This project was donated by Diamond Steel Construction Company, Commercial Piping Incorporated, Compco Metal Products Company, and the Campbell Construction Company.

Poplar vertical siding was installed over the deteriorated logs of the Camp Ranger's home.

The Order of the Arrow constructed the Personal Fitness Course.

1958- Members of Boy Scout Troop 16 of Struthers United Presbyterian Church worked hard planting 57 dogwood trees at Camp Stambaugh. The project, carried out by 26 Scouts and 3 leaders, gave Stambaugh its first dogwood trees, which were donated by Inglis Nursery. Wilfred Eisenbraun was Troop 16 Scoutmaster.

1962- A Long Range Plan was under way with an estimated cost of $436,000. The plan entailed major maintenance of Council properties including educational facilities for the office and staff, and new construction in Camp Stambaugh.

This Long Range Plan was first conceived in 1958 under the leadership of Council Executive Henry E. Katschke and Council President James L. Beeghly.

There were three committees to see the projects through completion: (1) Planning with Chairman G. Taylor Evans, Barclay M. Brandmiller MD., Paul Wick, Robert A. Manchester, Sidney S. Moyer, E.J. Salvidge, and M.Z. Bentley. (2) Action with Chairman Richard P.Shorts, Arnold D. Stambaugh, and James L. Beeghley. (3) Projects with Chairman Ralph I. Dillon, Walter S. Chuck, Mathew Johnson, Myron Ferguson, Wayne R. Stoyer, and Leo Poulakos.

Funds necessary for the plan were raised by finding individuals, clubs, and area businesses who would adopt a single project and finance it. A capital fund raising campaign was not held by the council. A regional staff representative told the executive board that the program would never get off the ground with this kind of an attitude on financing, but it did and very well! Projects were not approved until money to finish the job correctly were in the bank.

The most costly single project was the swimming pool and facilities.

The Long Range Plan of 1962 was one of the greatest demonstrations of Scouter cooperation, community endorsement, and support from area businesses and clubs.

With the exception of a few small items, the Long Range Plan of 1962 was completed in 1968. Projects completed included: the Swimming Pool and facilities (1963), the Sewage Disposal System (1963), the culvert bridge accessing the Marino Tract (1963), the campsites built on the Marino Tract (1964), residing of the Camp Ranger's Home with Poplar vertical siding (1965), extensive remodeling of the Wick Lodge, a New Eight Inch Well drilled 213 feet deep powered by a new three horse power pump to pump water to a new 3,000 gallon storage tank, building the Wallis Memorial Lodge (1965), and the Schwebel Memorial Lodge (1965),

acquiring Big Oak Wilderness Camp in Highlandtown (1963), building campsite washing and toilet facilities, building the Moyer Health Lodge (1967), building the Herb Hartzell Memorial Flag Platform (1967), improving the Marino Tract (1963-1964), and building a road to the White and Black Oaks campsites (1964).

A proposed new service center was part of the plan but was delayed.

Some estimated expenses follow:

Ranger's Home $5,000
Dining Hall 7,500
Wick Lodge 2,500
Council Ring Bleachers 5,000
Electric Power 5,000
Sewage Disposal 25,000
Water Well and Water Lines 20,000
Marino Tract Access 10,000
Road and Parking 3,500
Maintenance Machines 3,500
Swimming Pool and Facilities 85,000
Moyer Health Lodge 5,000
Wallis Memorial Lodge 7,000
Schwebel Memorial Lodge 7,000
Big Oak Wilderness Camp 100,000

CAMP HITCHCOCK. The council summer camp in 1918 was called "Camp Hitchcock". It was in the heart of Boardman Woods, which, in 1918, was over two miles away from everything.

The camp was hidden in deep, wild forest where there were many wild birds, animals, and a swimming hole.

Scouts camped for one week or more at $5.00 a week. The sessions ran Monday to Monday. K.F. Miller was camp director.

CAMP PROPERTIES. In 1919 Henry H. Stambaugh willed his 86½ acre Canfield farm to our council. It became known as "Camp Stambaugh".

In 1946, Marguerite and Rocco Marino donated 28½ acres known as the "Marino Tract" adjacent to Camp Stambaugh on the northeast corner.

In 1949, Arnold Stambaugh donated property in Pennsylvania to be used as high adventure "Explorer Camps". There were 80 acres in Crawford County and 43 acres in Mercer County. Both were sold later.

In 1963, Mr. and Mrs. Arnold Stambaugh donated 422 acres in Highlandtown Ohio to be used for the "Big Oak Wilderness Camp". It was sold later.

In 1975, an agreement was made with trustees from the Swanston property adjacent to Camp Stambaugh to use part of their land for "Camp Akela" Cub Day Camp.

In 1985, our council increased camp acreage by purchasing 270.63 acres of the Swanston property from Raccoon Road to the adjacent west side of "Camp Stambaugh".

CAMP RANGERS. The Stambaugh Scout Reservation always had a special person who could do just about anything from identify bugs and plants to repair machinery and cabins.

RANGERS AT CAMP STAMBAUGH	
1919-1922	Harry Wick (3 years)
1922-1945	Harry A. Walker (23 years)
1945-1951	Bob Kling (6 years)
1952-1955	Gene Brown (4 years)
1955-1979	Don Mikkelson* (24 years)
1980-1982	John Wilkenson (3 years)
1982-1983	Robert Gingery (2 years)
1983-present	Ross Lucarell*

* Mikkelson and Lucarell were the only two to attend National Ranger Training.

For almost 61 years, from 1919 to 1980, the location

of the old farm house (1919-1945) and log home (1947-present) at the entrance to the Stambaugh Scout Reservation served as home for the camp rangers and their families.

In 1980, the log home became the council office and from 1980-1983, camp rangers lived in the Moyer Health Lodge.

In 1983, Ranger Ross Lucarell and his family moved into the farm house on Raccoon Road which is part of the Camp Stambaugh property.

CAMP SEWAGE DISPOSAL SYSTEM. This system was placed in operation in 1963. It operates 24 hours a day all year servicing the Camp Ranger's Home (now the council office), public toilets that were under the K.L. Brown Pavilion, Meinecke Lodge, Wick Lodge, Katschke Lodge, and swimming pool toilets and showers.

CAMP STAMBAUGH. This was Henry H. Stambaugh's farm, and often referred to as the Stambaugh Farm. There was a farm house, a sheep barn, a red horse and hay barn and chicken coop. It was a well kept cultivated farm of 86½ acres with many fruit trees. It in no way resembled the woodlands which cover the acreage today. There was an operating oil well on the farm located behind the log gatehouse at the entrance to camp.

After Henry Stambaugh's death in 1919, his last will and testament dated November 14, 1918 provided the following: "I (Henry Stambaugh) give, devise and bequeath to PHILLIP J. THOMPSON, Trustee, for the use and benefit of the local Association of the BOY SCOUTS OF AMERICA, my farm in Canfield Township, known as Indian Creek Farm, containing about eighty six (86) acres of land...". Phillip J. Thompson and Henry Stambaugh owned the Stambaugh-Thompson Company. Thompson was very active with Scouting and served as Council President.

The farm house became the ranger's home and soon plans were under way to make use of the farm for camping.

The first official summer camp on the Stambaugh Farm was in 1919. (see "First Summer Camp At Stambaugh"). It operated for 12 days at a cost of $8.95 per Scout. A steel building was donated by Truscon Steel Company to be used as the camp kitchen. A large tent with mosquito netting was attached to the building to serve as the first dining hall.

In the fall of 1919, a small cabin was built on the north bank of the creek made of logs cut on the farm. It was named "Chief's Cabin" in honor of Council Executive Conrad Meinecke who designed and helped build the cabin.

No lake existed then. The pure clear water in the creek could be seen from the red barn at the top of the hill since the land was not heavily wooded.

Also in the fall the sheep barn, that was located in the area of the Emil Rauschenbach Memorial Flag Pole was moved down the hill on skids using a Model-T Ford. The farm was mostly open land. The barn was attached to the steel kitchen and served as the dining hall for the first time in the summer of 1920.

The "Stambaugh Farm" became known as the "Stambaugh Scout Reservation". Today it is called "Camp Stambaugh".

In 1946, 28½ acres of land was donated by Marguerite and Rocco Marino. This became known as the "Marino Tract". The Elm, Chestnut, and Locust campsites were developed on the Marino Tract.

Camp improvement projects took place through the years. (see "Camp Improvement"). Most of the hard work, equipment, and much of the materials were donated by committed Scouts, Scouters and friends of Scouting.

As part of the 1947 camp improvement, the K.L. Brown Pavilion replaced the farm's red hay barn using the same foundation. During the 1920s, a horse named Barney that came with the farm, was housed in the lower back section of the barn. Barney was used around camp for a few years. He pulled a wood scoop that was used by Camp Ranger Harry Walker in 1922 to enlarge a swimming hole along Indian Creek.

Also in 1947, a log cabin was built on the same site of the farm house that burned down in 1945.

In 1975, an agreement was made with trustees of the adjacent land known as the Swanston property to use a portion for what became known as "Camp Akela" for the Cub Day Camp Program.

In 1985, the Swanston property of 270.63 acres was purchased by our council.

Summer camp programs have gone from one 12-day session in 1919 to ten one-week sessions during 1967-1971. In the 1950s, there were eight weeks of camp. Recently camp has operated four weeks each summer.

Types of camping used throughout the years were: Pioneer, Troop, Provisional, Long Term, Camp, Explorer, and Stockade. Primarily the "Troop" plan has been used since 1949.

Campsites used throughout the years were: Aspen, Beech Knob, Black Oaks, Chestnut, Elm, Locust, Maple, Pines, White Oaks, Wild Apple, and Wild Cherry.

Since a national standard rating was developed to evaluate summer camp operation, Camp Stambaugh always received an "A" rating with the exception of one year. Then in 1990, National changed the rating process from levels of A, B, and C, to either meeting National accreditation standards or not.

Summer camp attendance went from less than 200 Scouts in 1919 to 600 Scouts in 1949, to 1,200 Scouts in 1971. It was estimated in 1971, that some 500,000 Scouts had used Camp Stambaugh for summer and week-end camping. Today enrollment for summer camp is less than 400 Boy Scouts and 450 Cub Scouts each year.

During the 1950s and part of the 1960s, a pre-camp camporee week-end was held at Camp Stambaugh to give the Scouts a preview of the summer camp program.

Throughout the years there have been the following cabins: Baden Powell (24 people), Chief's (Pioneer, 6 people), Eagle's (for Eagle Scouts, 8 people), Neff's Eagle Cabin (6 people), Hoover (24 people), Hunter (15 people), McKinley (12 people), Moyer (4 people), Schwebel (24 people), Strouss (14 people), Teddy Roosevelt (8 people), Walker (14 people), Wallis (24 people), and the Telescope cabin.

When you rented a cabin, they were equipped with double deck cots and mattresses or bed sacks filled with straw in the earlier days. During the 1950s, the Hoover, McKinley, and Hunter cabins were equipped with dishes and cooking utensils. All had electricity except for the Pioneer cabin.

Summer camp cost in 1919 was $8.95 for 12-days. In 1992 summer camp cost was $95.00 for 7-days.

CAMP THOMPSON. Phillip J. Thompson was Council President from 1914 to 1917. During his administration the First Council Camp was opened in 1914 on the E.J. McCullough Farm on the Poland-New Springfield Road. The camp was known as "Camp Thompson". The campsite was located on Yellow Creek that ran through the farm. A huge maple tree provided shade. An old cabin that was repaired was in the camping area and used by the Scouts. This camp was used by the Youngstown Scouts as a council summer camp from 1914-1917.

CAMPSITE TROOP KITCHEN. Sometime in the 1930s-1940s, small four sided screened buildings were built in campsites used as troop kitchens. Troops not using the dining hall would cook meals outside the troop kitchen and eat inside. Later these buildings were used for nature lodges in the summer and storage in the winter. Only one still stands today near the adirondaks.

CHAPEL IN CAMP STAMBAUGH. A chapel was located in the woods to the right of the road that goes down the hill from the parking lot. Just below the flat area where Emil Raushenbaugh's flag pole is. It had saplings lashed together for a backdrop and a small podium made of brick. Simple benches were in the ground made of upright logs with planks across the top of the logs. This chapel was built in 1963. There were many mosquitoes since this area was very damp and enclosed by pine trees.

In 1970, an inter-faith A-frame chapel was built on the north bank of Indian Creek. A fund campaign raised money for the project. It was designed and built by Walter Damon.

The support beams came from a razed barn. Dedication took place July 14, 1971 under the combined authority of the Council's Protestant and Catholic Committees on Scouting.

Several different articles on the chapel read that it was dedicated in memory of all departed Scouters. Another read it is a tribute to those who have given so much in the service of boyhood. And yet another read it was built to honor the past and to inspire the future.

On the flier that was used to generate funds for the project, it stated: "The name of each person to be honored and remembered will be placed on a dignified Memorial device which will become a part of the chapel". That never happened.

CHAPLAINS IN CAMP STAMBAUGH. The camp chaplain's responsibility is to assist Boy Scouts in working for Scouting's religious awards and to conduct non-denominational vesper services. They also counsel those in need and serve as a member of the summer camp staff.

The first full-time chaplain for Camp Stambaugh summer camp staff was hired in 1969. He was 23 year old Ray Thomas, a second year theology student at Mt. Saint Mary Seminar. He attended camp school training for chaplains at Camp Beaumont in Rock Creek before summer camp opened on June 22. Both the diocese and Boy Scout Council shared in the costs and salary. Since then, Ray has been ordained a Catholic Priest.

I remember serving on Staff with Ray. He certainly was the right man for the job. He had the patience of a saint and was one of those guys everyone liked.

Besides his regular duties, he also handled home sick cases. Some weeks the Scouts and even some staff members kept Ray busy all day and sometimes at night. He enjoyed his job. But now that I think of it, one day he did ask me if I would switch jobs with him! I was lakefront director that year.

According to the Reverend Norman M. Parr, D.D., executive director of the Council of Churches at that time, Thomas' appointment was the second ecumenical venture of its type in America. Prior to this time, there were no chaplain staff members on camp staff. A religious person would only visit the camp on a regular basis in order to provide religious services. Priests and ministers had, for a long time, wanted a full-time chaplain available in Scout camps on a 24 hour a day basis.

Catholic laymen who served on the chaplaincy steering committee included chairman Edward Holmes, treasurer Franklin Ernst, and secretary Dennis Wilde. It was agreed that a different religion be represented each year.

The local Catholic Committee on Scouting later paid the salary for Camp Stambaugh summer camp chaplains.

Other chaplains who served at Stambaugh on a part-time or full-time basis were: Protestant William Maloney and Catholic Stephen Dimoff in 1955 and Sam DiCioccio in 1971.

CHASE, JOHN G. He served as volunteer Scout Commissioner from 1911 to 1918. He was a motivating spirit behind the Scouting program in Youngstown. He served as volunteer Council Executive from April 1, 1913 when the council became chartered until August of 1916 when a professional Council Executive was hired.

He was an able botanist and astronomer and worked as the director of the Youngstown Playground Association for the city.

During a camporee in Wick Park in June of 1943, Scouts built an ornamental fireplace as a memorial to John H. Chase. Two hundred Scouts were in attendance.

CHIEF'S CABIN. The Chief's Cabin was the first structure to be built on the Stambaugh Scout Reservation in 1919 by Scouts and leaders. It was a one room log cabin measuring about 20x15 feet, and constructed of trees cut in camp. It was built about 30 feet from Indian Creek on the north shore. There wasn't a lake then. A fireplace inside was used for cooking and heating.

The cabin was named "Chief's Cabin" for Conrad Meinecke who was our first Council Executive. He designed the lodge and helped build it.

Meinecke conducted many organizational meetings in this cabin with local and national Scout leaders to sculpture the future of the Boy Scout program in our council. Meinecke and his family lived in the cabin during the summer months.

In 1920, a mud hole was dug east of the cabin along the creek. This created a small pond for the Scouts to swim in. Also during this year, the name "Chief's Cabin" was changed to "Pioneer Cabin".

An underground cooler for storing food was dug into the side of the hill behind the cabin.

In 1930, a diving platform was built near the cabin so Scouts who were swimmers could dive into the lake.

In later years, the Aquatic staff lived in this cabin during summer camp. The staff painted a large sea horse on the door of the cabin during the 1950s.

As part of the Camp Stambaugh Capital Improvement program in early 1955, a boat dock was built in front of the Chief's Cabin.

The cabin was taken down in 1961 because of decay.

After Conrad E. Meinecke left our council, he wrote two books of which one was titled, "Your Cabin In The Woods". There are two pages of plans for the "Chief's Cabin" in the book. See "Meinecke, Conrad".

CHRIST MISSION CAMP. In 1949, a children's health group chosen by visiting nurses of Youngstown, opened a nine-week camping program at a camp that was located just west of Camp Stambaugh and Camp Akela on Leffingwell Road. Tony Vivo was Camp Director then. The camp cared for 250 boys over the summer camping season. Eight counselors and nurses were on duty. A new swimming pool was used for about 90 percent of their program. Other activities included attendance at Youngstown Athletics Baseball games, visits to parks in the area, and theatrical plays given at the camp by various local organizations.

COAL IN CAMP. Behind the Walker Cabin at the bottom of the hill was an outcropping of coal. This coal was dug out and brought up the hill with a horse and wagon along a road that lead down to the coal area from the area that is now known as the Beech Knob campsite. The coal was used in the cabins for heating during the winter months around the 1940s and 1950s.

COMING OF AGE JAMBOREE. In August of 1929, a great "Coming of Age Jamboree" of Scouts of all countries assembled at Birkenhead, England. A delegation of 11 Scouts and leaders led by Earl Haefner, Scoutmaster of Troop 15, and Chief Harry Hunter represented the Mahoning Valley Council.

CONSOLIDATION TALKS IN 1986. Discussion to consolidate or merge Mahoning Valley Council with another council has been evident since the 1940s. But it wasn't until 1984 when Mahoning Valley Council's Council Executive Theodore Parker initiated talks between Mahoning Valley Council and Western Reserve Council in Warren. Financial concern was the reason for consolidation consideration.

Actual investigation and negotiation didn't take place until 1986.

It is important to understand the difference between consolidation and merging. Consolidation is when two councils dissolve their identities and form one new council under a new name. Merging is when one council dissolves its identity and is absorbed by another council taking on the absorbing council's name and identity.

The reason for considering consolidation of Mahoning Valley Council and Western Reserve Council were (1) both were small councils and combining them would be more cost effective, (2) one council office and service center for both areas could benefit the Scouts and Scouters better with a larger supply of inventory in one geographically centered location, this location would have been Liberty Township, (3) a larger number of qualified professionals could be hired to support units and to service more youth in both areas.

"When you pool your resources, you're bound to do better. In the long run, consolidation will be to both councils' advantage." said Perry Hesselman, president of the Western Reserve Council.

"If you take any two medium sized companies, you can put them together and build a stronger company," remarked Mike Russell, president of the Mahoning Valley Council.

Russell was a member of the consolidation study committee. He noted, "In three years of sitting on this committee, no one could give a solid reason for objecting to the consolidation. Some said they just don't like it."

For about three years, both councils' executive boards had sub-committees to investigate the possibilities and value of consolidation. Both councils' executive boards voted to continue consolidation efforts since it would be of value to Scouting in these two areas, from a business point of view.

Mahoning Valley Council officers during this time were: Council Executive Theodore Parker (1984), Council Executive Fred Baird (1984-1993) succeeded Parker after Parker's death in 1984, Council President Charles Cushwa (1985), Council President Michael Russell (1986-1987), and Council President Dr. David Ritchie (1988).

Information regarding the consolidation proposal was given to the registered members of each council as talks progressed.

On June 2 of 1988, Western Reserve Executive Board members and volunteer leaders who were eligible to vote, voted on the consolidation. It was defeated primarily by the volunteer leaders.

Mahoning Valley Council's members were to vote June 9th but canceled that meeting as a result of Western Reserve Council's decision. Dr. Ritchie was quoted to say, "The facts have been given to the Scouters, and I can't really say very many have come out against it [consolidation]."

Even though both councils' executive boards were in favor of the consolidation, volunteers in both councils refused it because of their concern for their Scout camps; Mahoning Valley's Camp Stambaugh in Canfield and Western Reserve's Camp Chicagomi in Parkman.

"From day one," Russell said emphatically, "it was agreed both camps could and would be utilized. There was no thought we would sell either camp."

It was noted that diversity of camp locations would be a plus. Camp Chickagami, the smaller of the two, is flat while Camp Stambaugh has rolling hills. Alternate use of both camps would offer a more appealing camping program and the acreage would be needed to accommodate council membership.

Both Council Executives Fred Baird of Mahoning Valley and Marc Posner of Western Reserve agreed they would need both camps in order to service the Cub Scout and Boy Scout programs.

CONSOLIDATION TALKS IN 1992. Early in 1992, consolidation talks came alive again. Pressure from the National office to consolidate was strong now. Small councils in the country found it impossible to meet the high requirement demands for rechartering and to generate the needed funds to operate.

Along with Mahoning Valley Council and Western Reserve Council, Northeast Ohio Council in Painesville was being considered this time.

On February 10, 1993, all three councils voted to consolidate together into one new council under the temporary name of "Steel Valley Council" until an adequate name is selected.

COUNCIL EXECUTIVES. The Youngstown Council was started in 1911 and chartered April 1, 1913. Prior to 1916, volunteer administrators guided the development of the Youngstown Boy Scout Council.
The following have served as Council Executives:

1916-1917	John Cross
1917-1923 ...(6 years)................	Conrad E. Meinecke
1923-1936 ...(13 years)................	Harry H. Hunter
1936-1949 ...(13 years)...............	Kenneth L. Brown
1949-1968 ...(19 years)..............	Henry E. Katschke
1968-1974 ...(6 years)...............	Dean Johnson
1974-1985 ...(10 years)................	Ted Parker
1985-1993 ...(8 years)................	Fred Baird

COUNCIL NEWSLETTERS. The first council newsletter was prepared in 1917 by Council Executive Conrad Meinecke. It was two 8½x11 inch sheets of paper typed and fastened together.

In the 1950s the newsletter was named "The Totem Pole".

In February of 1969, the council published its first professionally typeset and printed publication with pictures. It took the form of an 11x17 inch sheet folded in half with sometimes a single sheet insert. This style met with much approval on the part of the leaders.

The council during this time always exchanged bulletins with other councils.

Around 1980, the council was preparing the council newsletter in the office. In short, it resembled the one sent in 1917!

In 1985 I made a remark to Council Executive Fred Baird about the quality of the newsletter. Fred said, "if you have any suggestions or could help us to improve the newsletter, I'd be happy to listen". So I thought, "Why not a real newspaper".

Fred and I met over lunch one afternoon a week later. I said, "Fred, what do you think about a real newspaper with lots of pictures?" Fred's eyes lit up. "Wow. Who's going to typeset it?" He said, "I will on my new computer" I said. Fred continued with, "Who's going to pay for the printing cost?" After thinking for a minute and not wanting this idea to fail, I answered. "I'll get ads from area businesses".

As it ended up, I became the reporter, photographer, advertising sales manager typesetter, and mail room manager for the new tabloid "Totem Pole". And I enjoyed every minute of it.

An issue was published every other month from December 1985 through December 1987. There were anywhere from 4 to 16 pages.

A special thanks goes to Joe Angelo Sr. for helping to recruit advertisers and Terry Lee Mock for helping in the mailing preparations.

From 1988-1993, the council newsletter was published in the council office again. The format was 8½x14 inch sheet folded in half to form a booklet.

The council newsletter has taken many forms during the years, but always with the thought in mind of informing our membership and interested public.

The extensive mailing list to members and interested public and businesses have helped to generate a lot of good will.

COUNCIL OFFICE. 1916-1917. The first official council office was desk space in the Chamber of Commerce.

1917-1927. In late November, the office was moved to the southwest corner of the basement of the Reuben-McMillan Library located at the corner of Wick and Rayen Avenues.

1928-1931. Since the Boy Scout program was growing, more office space was needed. On December 22, 1927, the council office moved to the second floor rooms above the Metropolitan Savings and Loan Association (also listed as Pfau-Paige Auto Company) at 217 Wick Avenue.

1931-1941. The council office moved to the rooms at the Salow building on N. Phelps Street.

1941-1949. The council office moved to the King Funeral Home at 120 East Rayen Avenue. The council rented this building until purchasing it in 1949. The down payment was made by a donation from the Youngstown-Foundation and Mr. C.J. Strouss, Sr.

1949-1975. On July 24th in 1949, the council purchased the King funeral home at 120 East Rayen Avenue for $10,000. Improvements were made to the interior and the upstairs was rented to the Girl Scout Council with their entrance at 118 East Rayen Avenue.

In the early 1950s, the outside of the building was remodeled with much of the old style ginger-bread construction removed.

While renting this building, the council office didn't have janitor service. Waste paper baskets were emptied in the basement and it was piled high. Rats and mice were thick in the building.

There was a home behind the office that was included in the purchase. This home was occupied by Mr. & Mrs. Timothy Shea and daughter, Dorothy Shea.

With approval from the council executive board, Council Executive Henry Katschke visited with the Sheas about becoming the office janitors. The board agreed that they would have their rent free and the council paid them $35 per month beginning November 1, 1949.

Cleaning the council office became a family affair. They did an outstanding service to the council.

Dorothy Shea took over the cleaning service from her parents and at the time of printing this book, Dorothy continues the cleaning service for the council office. The Shea family has been the one and only janitor service the council has had.

1975-1980- In May of 1975, a new council office was built at 3691 LeHarps Road at a cost of $108,000.

They moved in May 1, 1975 and dedicated June 15th. LeHarps is off of Meridian near Route 680.

1980-present. After Camp Ranger Don Mikkelson retired, the ranger's home at the top of the hill in Camp Stambaugh became the council office in January.

COUNCIL PRESIDENTS. The Youngstown Council was started in 1911 and chartered April 1, 1913.

The following have served as Council Presidents:

1913	George L. Fordyce
1914-1917	Phillip J. Thompson
1918	James L. Wick,Jr.
*	
1920-1921	Edmond S. Brown
1922	E. Mason Wick
1923-1924	Dr. C.C. Booth
1925-1929	Myron C. Wick,Jr.
1930	G.F. Hammond
1931-1936	Paul Wick
*	
1947	Paul Wick
1948-1953	Robert A. Manchester
1954-1956	G. Taylor Evans
1957-1959	James L. Beeghly
1960-1962	David E. Carroll
1963	H.B. Gould
1964-1965	William T. Storey
1966-1967	Jay C. Brownlee
1968-1969	Frank K. Stillwagon
1970-1972	Henry J. McNicholas
1973	William G. Lyden,Jr.
1974-1977	Russell Bungar
1978	Dave Gundry/Russ Bungar
1979	Fred Bailey
*	
1984-1985	Charles Cushwa,III
1986-1987	Michael Russell
1988-1989	Dr. David Ritchie
1990-1991	Ron DiTosto
1992-1993	Dr. Michael Woloschak

The first man of Catholic faith to serve as council president was William T. Storey in 1964-1965.

COUNCIL RING. The council ring is a place where campers and guests get together in camp, usually at the end of a day, to sing songs, perform, tell stories or have ceremonies. A council fire is built on what could be termed the stage area.

The Stambaugh Scout Reservation had a natural amphitheater on the property. It was an old limestone quarry left from the farm days. Just north of the creek, it provided a perfect location for the camp council ring. Throughout the history of camp, this area has always been the main council ring.

In 1919, terraces were carved into the hillside and used for seating through 1929. Those attending sat on the hillside. On the outside of each terrace was a half buried horizontal log to help prevent washout. Some Scouters recall sitting on the dirt terrace seat with their knees bent and feet resting on the logs. Later logs were placed upright in the ground on the terraces. Scouts would sit on top of the short logs. Not too comfortable!

At a dedication on Thursday evening, July 20, 1950, the Youngstown Rotary Club presented new bleachers for the council ring with a seating capacity of 1,000 people. The grandstand construction was made of wood and rested in concrete into the hill overlooking the council ring. This was the first time proper seating was built in this major area of camp.

In 1970, Council Executive Dean Johnson was interested in building new bleachers in the council ring. The grandstands that were there from 1950 had decayed. Johnson was now looking for bleachers that had removable seats so they could be stored during the winter months. Upon seeking bids for the job, he found the price tag to be over $14,000. The project never took place.

COUNCIL STAFF IN 1949. The council professional staff consisted of a council executive, assistant council executive, and 3 district executives for 10 districts. Later the staff was enlarged to 8 men, 5 women, and 1 camp ranger.

COUNTY SCOUT ORGANIZATION. Steps were taken in 1919 to form a County Scout Organization. A committee representing the various townships met with the Council Executive Board. The County Committee was composed of Jerome Hull, T.J. Mayers, Harry A. Walker, R.C. Druhot, and Ernest Huntley. The council named as its representatives; Frank Herrick, J.M. Hanson, Dr. A.C. Tidd, and Chief Meinecke (the Council Executive).

CROSS, JOHN Cross was hired on August 13, 1916, as the first Council Executive but lasted less than a year before he was released. He was a big softy from Columbus, Kansas who was recommended by National Headquarters.

(1) David E. Carroll, Council President, 1960-1962. (photo by Lee Banks). **(2)** Bart Ingram, Camp Director, 1967-1971. **(3)** Ray Thomas, Catholic Seminarian in 1969 became the first full-time summer camp chaplain. (photo by author). **(4)** Edward Cook. (photo by Lee Banks, 1965). **(5-6)** Camp Chapel: (5) 1960s, (6) 1971-1993. (photos 5 & 6 by Jerry Stanovcak). **(7-9)** Council office: **(7)** at 120 East Rayen Avenue, 1955 in the old King Funeral Home; **(8)** as the camp ranger's home before 1980, built 1947 replacing the farm house; **(9)** 1993. (photo by author).

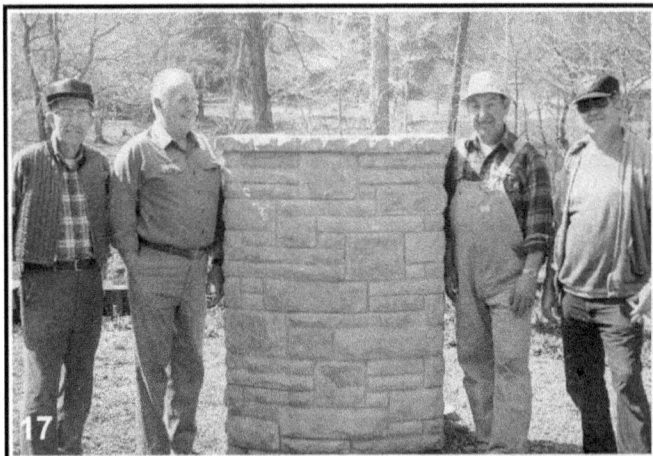

(10) Stambaugh farm house on Leffingwell Road, 1919.
(11) Behind the farm house, (a) red hay barn (replaced by the K.L Brown Pavilion), (b) chicken coop (Rotary Building today), (c) sheep barn that became the dining hall. (photos 10 & 11, by Vindicator, 1919). **(12)** Red hay barn at the entrance into camp, 1931. (photo from 16mm movie). **(13)** Chief's cabin on the north side of the lake, 1928. (Cook album). **(14)** Underground cooler behind Chief's cabin, 1928. **(15)** Council Executives (from left) Henry E. Katschke, Kenneth L. Brown, and Harry H. Hunter near the Chief's cabin, 1949. **(16)** Sitting against the Council Fire Ring backdrop in 1954, (from left) John Dodge, Henry Katschke, Bob Summers, and A.D. Hamilton. (photo by Lee Banks). **(17)** Speakers podium in the Council Fire Ring, 1979. From left: Charles McNatt, Council Executive Ted Parker, podium builder Donald Baumgartner, and Judge Fred Bailey. (photo by Vindicator).

DANIEL BOONE BUILDING. From the mid 1920s until 1931 a building stood near the lake up the hill just west of where the Wick Lodge was built. This was called the Daniel Boone. The building was half enclosed and half opened under one roof. Units would camp in tents around the structure, cook under the open pavilion half of the building and eat their meals inside the enclosed half.

DEPRESSION YEARS. The depression years of the 1930s proved to be a period of continued advance for Mahoning Valley Council, in spite of the economic conditions which made necessary a decreased budget. The Stambaugh Reservation was made self supporting for the first time in its history and 19% of the Scouts participated in summer camp.

DINING HALL. When the Stambaugh Reservation was ready to open for its first official summer camp in 1919, the Truscon Steel Company donated a steel building that became the camp kitchen. A large tent was attached to it where the campers and leaders ate their meals. This served as the first dining hall.

The Stambaugh farm had an old pine constructed sheep barn where Henry Stambaugh housed his sheep. The barn was located at the top of the hill near where the Emil Rauschenbach Memorial Flag pole is today.

In the fall of 1919, after the first summer camp operation took place on the Stambaugh Reservation, several ambitious Scouters and neighboring farmers, with limited funds, used a model-T Ford and skids to move the sheep barn to the bottom of the hill. Most of the Stambaugh farm at that time was open fields and apple orchards. This made the move possible. The farm back then in no way resembled the plush wooded land that exists today.

Once moved, the sheep barn was attached to the steel kitchen to replace the tent. This became the camp dining hall and gathering place.

The dining hall was named, "Meinecke Lodge" after Council Executive Conrad Meinecke who was a creative builder and assisted in the dining hall construction.

An open porch was built around the barn in the spring of 1920 to provide more room. Rolled up canvas flaps hung on the outer side of the porch and could be dropped during inclement weather. By the summer camp season of 1920, the Meinecke Lodge was ready to serve as the camp dining hall.

During the following early years of the 1920s, a fireplace was built on the west wall of the barn. By the last half of the 1920s, the canvas flaps were replaced with a permanent wall. Wood burning heaters were also added.

Through the 1930s and 1940s, the Meinecke Lodge remained much the same.

From January through May of 1950, the Meinecke Lodge underwent major re-construction and prepared for winter use, thanks to money donated by the Elks Lodge, Lions Club of Youngstown, and Mrs. Clarence Strouss, Sr.

The kitchen store room was added to the back southwest corner of the kitchen. The fireplace inside the main room was removed. The cement fireplace foundation under the floor of the lodge can still be seen. An attic ladder replaced the chimney through the ceiling. New outer walls and windows were built. Maintenance or replacement was made on kitchen equipment. Many individuals and companies contributed equipment, money and man-hours.

Prior to 1950 in the off-season, campers slept upstairs in the loft and gathered downstairs for fellowship near the huge fireplace.

In 1951, for the first time recorded, the Meinecke Lodge was rented to non-Scout groups for $25.00. The capacity was listed at 150 people.

In the fall of 1955, major improvement projects took place on the Meinecke Lodge again. The Truscon Steel Company donated a new metal building to replace the one they donated in 1919 that became badly rusted. Construction was performed with volunteer help. Material cost was $2000.

Adequate hot water was always a problem at camp Stambaugh prior to the 1955 improvements. The small hot water heater used in the dining hall supplied all the hot water for dishwashing, kitchen use and the nearby shower house. When the new kitchen was constructed in 1955, a proper new hot water system was installed and the plumbing was replaced. Estimated cost of the project was $1500.

Proper and adequate dishwashing equipment was also installed at a cost of $1800. The dishwasher that was in service from 1950-1955 was adequate at the time since there were only 75 Scouts per week in camp. But after 1955, the dishwasher became outdated with some of the camping periods having as many as 180 campers to feed at one time. Dishwashing became an "all day" (and sometimes night) job.

Food storage was always a real problem at Camp Stambaugh until the Century Food Company supplied the camp with an eight-foot cooler with all the necessary equipment and safety devices. Cost of installation was $87.

On May 12, 1956, heavy rains caused the dam to wash out and high water undermined the foundation of the Meinecke Lodge.

The furnace to heat the lodge was added sometime in the 1970s by Lou Cicchillo, a long time volunteer Scouter and furnace specialist.

In 1987, the Properties Committee recommended to the Council Executive Board that a new dining hall be considered for the near future because the Meinecke Lodge was rapidly deteriorating. The same original beams from the sheep barn of 1919 still serve as the framework of the lodge today. No one knows how many years before 1919 the sheep barn was built.

Under the direction of Council President Michael Russell during his term of office from 1986-1987, and Council Executive Frederick Baird, the Council Executive Committee began raising money for a new dining hall.

In 1989, plans were approved to build a new dining hall in Camp Stambaugh. The Rotary Club contributed to the project and various area companies and vocational organizations assisted with the construction in order to reduce the costs. Under the leadership of Council Board and Rotary Club member Don Hall, construction of the building was completed in 1992 but did not go into service that year. Estimated costs including donated labor, equipment, and material was $300,000.

DISTRICTS WITHIN THE COUNCIL. When the council first began in 1911, it operated as one territory. As the Scouting program grew, the council was divided into smaller territories and assigned a volunteer leader known as a commissioner, similar to today.

By 1927, Sebring was added to the council.

In 1931, the council was divided into districts and subdivided into divisions.

By 1935, there were nine geographic sub-divisions each headed by a volunteer leader. These divisions and volunteer leaders were:

Northern Division .... E.P. Gilronan
Southern Division .... W.E. Slagle
Eastern Division .... Ralph Hawkins
Western Division .... Frank Bertch
Central Division .... Cy Firth
Suburban District .... Ray Pugh
Southeastern Division .... Norman Ellis

Struthers/Lowellville District .... Les Lee
Hubbard District .... George Ferver
By 1949, the Council was operating with 10 districts.

Early in 1950, Paul Wick served as chairman of a special committee to reduce the council's ten districts to six.

In 1952, the six districts were reduced to five. Through the 1950s, 1960s, and 1970s, the council belonged to Region IV in the National organization which consisted of Ohio, Kentucky and West Virginia totaling 37 councils in 1962 out of 530 councils in the United States.

Mahoning Valley Council consisted of Mahoning County and townships of Hubbard, Palmyra, and Deerfield.

Sometime in the 1970s, the council reorganized into three districts.

Towards the end of 1985, the council was reduced from three districts to two.

Through the years district names included: Arrowhead, Big Arrow, Big Waters, Council Rock, Pioneer, Tomahawk, and Western Reserve.

Then in February of 1986, due to reduced membership, the council was reorganized again into one district named, "Stambaugh District".

DOGWOOD TREES PLANTED AT CAMP. Members of Boy Scout Troop 16 of Struthers United Presbyterian Church with Scoutmaster Wilfred Eisenbraun worked hard planting 57 dogwood trees at Camp Stambaugh in 1958. The project was carried out by 26 Scouts and 3 leaders. This was Camp Stambaugh's first dogwood trees. The trees were donated by Inglis Nursery.

DRUM AND BUGLE CORPS. The first council Drum and Bugle Corps was organized early in 1919. Forty nine boys were present at the first meeting.

In 1928, the Drum and Bugle Corps was reorganized under the direction of William Armstrong. Two years later, David C. Evans was named field commissioner in charge of the corps.

In 1930, the Drum & Bugle Corp became eligible for the Musicians Award.

In the early 1930s, Carl E. Quinn Jr. became deputy director and set a goal to have 20 trained drummers.

(1-16) Dining Hall: **(1)** 1919, getting ready for the first official summer camp. **(2)** 1919, the dining tent. **(3)** 1920, an open porch was added to the sheep barn. **(4)** Late 1920s, permanent walls, windows, wood heaters and fireplace were added. **(5)** 1920, camp kitchen with cook "Aunt Ethel Johnson". **(6)** Late 1920s, Scouters and board members sit facing the fireplace while guitars and banjos were played. Entrance to kitchen is at left. (photos 1-6, Robert Manchester album). **(7)** 1949, note the shower house to the far right. **(8)** 1949, back view. Shower house is seen at left. **(9)** 1955, backview. (photo by Spratt Studio). **(10)** 1950, a Scout leader climbed the flagpole to take this photo. **(11)** 1931, Harry Walker by the fireplace. Porch behind fireplace was enclosed for storage. (Ed Cook album). **(12)** 1950, removal of the fireplace. **(13)** July 1971, from left: Don Reuter, Richard Rice, Don Ruse, and Camp Director Bart Ingram. **(14)** 1949, summer camp trading post window on east side of dining hall. Entrance to loft is in background. (photos 7,8,10,12,14 by Henry Katschke). **(15)** 1969 kitchen crew, from left: Larry DeCamp, Troop 145; Dave Jockman, Troop 50; & Leonard Paskevich, Troop 93. (Vindicator). **(16)** 1984, from left: Sandra Romano, Camp Director Jeff Dyer, Camp Cook "Mama Romano". (photo by author). **(17)** Council President Ron DiTosto (1990-1991). **(18)** Council Commissioner Robert Davis (1980s-1993). (photos 17,18 by Jack Acri, 1988). **(19)** Circa 1920s, Reuben-McMillan Library before Scouts hike to Oak Hill Cemetery & Henry Stambaugh's grave. (vindicator).

EAGLE'S CABIN. This cabin was built by and for Eagle Scouts in the early 1920s. The cabin was the focus point of many stories. One story being that of "One Boot". Its been said that when the cabin was destroyed by fire, one of the occupants perished in the fire and his spirit roams the camp at night. Sometimes you can hear him coming. The sound he makes is like a heavy boot hitting the ground followed by the dragging of the other foot. It is known as "One Boot".

The cabin acquired names as "Eagle's Nest", "Eagle's Roost", and "Eagle's Peak".

EAGLE SCOUT BADGE. Ernest Thompson Seton was one of the founders of the Boy Scouts of America. It was his idea to call the highest Boy Scout rank the "Wolf Scout". But Dan Beard, the other founder of the Boy Scouts of America, was able to change the name to "Eagle Scout".

The first Eagle Scout badge was designed and illustrated in the 1911 Scout Handbook but was never made. A revised badge was made and on Labor Day in 1912, the first Eagle badge in the United States was awarded to Arthur R. Eldred, at age 16, of Troop #1 in Rockville Centre, Long Island, New York.

He advanced rapidly through the ranks becoming a First Class Scout by March 1911. By April 1912, he had completed the last of the 21 merit badges then required for Eagle.

To make sure that Arthur Eldred was worthy of the BSA's first Eagle badge, he was reviewed not only by his own troop's board of review but by a special board composed of the three major figures in Scouting, Chief Scout Executive James E. West, Chief Scout Ernest Thompson Seton, and National Scout Commissioner Dan Beard.

Because the die had not yet been cut for the Eagle badge, Arthur Eldred had to wait until Labor Day in 1912 to get the emblem of honor.

The Eagle Scout badge has seen many changes since its beginning.

All Eagle badges since its beginning in 1912 have a metal scroll that is turned up at its ends which symbolizes a Scout's smile. The words "Be Prepared" are inscribed on the scroll. A simple overhand knot which symbolizes "do a good turn daily", hangs from the center of the scroll. Attached to the back of the scroll is a hanging red, white, and blue ribbon with a ring at the bottom that is fastened to the metal Eagle badge.

From 1912 to the mid 1920s, there were variations and different sizes. Some had the Eagle's beak open, some were closed. In 1912, 1913, and 1914, the medals were cast in bronze, and in 1915, sterling silver medals were started and ended in 1979. Starting in 1980 maladium metal finished with non-tarnishing rhodium reduced the cost of casting the badge. It is less detailed because it does not cast as well as silver. The back of the Eagle badge was engraved with feathers all years except from the mid 1950s through 1971 where the back is smooth. The letters "BSA" appear across the front of the eagle on all badges except those made from the early 1930s through 1971. Embroidered cloth Eagle patches started in 1923. Embroidery was on a rectangular piece of green material from 1923 through the mid 1950s when the oval patch was made. Design on the patches changed six times.

In the first Americanized handbook for the Boy Scouts of America in 1911, requirements for the range of Eagle Scout read: "Any First-Class Scout qualifying for twenty-one merit badges will be entitled to wear the highest Scout merit badge. This is an eagle's head in silver, and represents the all around perfect Scout".

EAGLE SCOUT CLUB. The club was formed in 1924 and called "Epsilon Sigma Gamma". Its purpose was to aid Commissioners in their regular visits to troops and to assist weak troops. It was also a social club for Eagle Scouts.

The first club president was Ralph Bulla. Others that followed were: Roland Clarke, Finley Smith, William Campbell, Ray Bevan, and Arthur Thomas.

EAGLE SCOUTS IN OUR COUNCIL. The first presentation of the Eagle badge in our council took place June 2, 1920. Two Scouts from Troop 11 achieved the Eagle rank at the same time. The Scouts were Joseph Prall Morgan and Ellwood S. Harrar. Joseph Morgan became an attorney and president of the Bar Association in Youngstown. Ellwood S. Harrar's son, Dr. J. George Harrar who also earned the Eagle Rank later, became president of the Rockerfeller Foundation around 1962.

In 1926, three Youngstown Scouts had their Eagle Scout badge pinned on their breast by Sir Baden Powell in Detroit where Powell visited during his tour of the United States.

In 1930, forty-eight boys achieved the Eagle Rank setting a record for the council at that time.

At a conference in 1949 with the editors of the Vindicator, it was agreed that the picture and biographical sketch of each new Eagle Scout in the council would be published. The responsibility for getting the information to the Vindicator rested with the troop of which the boy was a member.

For the past several years, long time Scouter Jack Acri of Acri Photography has volunteered his service of photographing each Eagle Scout for the vindicator at no charge.

As of March 1, 1993, there have been 2455 Scouts awarded the Eagle badge in Mahoning Valley Council.

ENTERLINE, ED K. Ever since I have known Ed Enterline, he was always on some worldwide Scouting trip to Australia, New Zealand or other overseas location. He always had an interesting story to tell us. Ed was Scoutmaster of Troop 30 in Canfield.

EVANS, G. TAYLOR. He was chairman of the planning committee for the "Long Range Plan of 1962". In 1954, while council president, he established the practice of a council president not serving more than a three year term in office. Prior, there was no limitation.

EXECUTIVE COMMITTEE, 1916. Executive Committee members were Henry A. Butler, James P. Collerah, Hugh W. Grant, Frank Herrick, Harry Levinson, I. Harry Meyer, Philip J. Thompson, and James L. Wick Jr.

They decided to have the Rotary Club raise money for the first full-time Scout Executive in 1916.

EXPLORER BOWLING TOURNAMENT. This event was created by the Explorer Cabinet during the 1960s and sponsored each spring by the B'nai B'rith Lodge. The lodge made available trophies for individuals and posts. A rotating "top" trophy was awarded to the winning post each year.

EXPLORER CAMP IN PENNSYLVANIA. Arnold D. Stambaugh, vice-president of Mahoning Valley Boy Scout Council, gave 123 acres of forest land to our Explorer Scouts as a Christmas gift on December 24th, 1949. The land was in Pennsylvania approximately 25 miles from Youngstown in Crawford and Mercer counties. The 120 acres consisted of one 43 acre tract and one 80 acre tract.

Stambaugh presented the property deed to the council at a noon meeting of the executive committee at the Y.M.C.A. Richard Owsley, chairman of the Explorer

Division accepted the gift on behalf of the council.

Explorers during this time often took camping trips into unexplored territory where they roughed it.

EXPLORER CAMP PROGRAM. From July 1 to 8 in 1951, 34 Explorer Scouts took part in a special summer camp program. It was the first of its kind at the Stambaugh Reservation.

The purpose was to furnish a program for young men who have been to the regular summer camp as Boy Scouts. It was designed to help them plan and carry out the Explorer program for boys ages 14-16 in their own units.

EXPLORER CANOE RACE. The first canoe race for Explorers took place in Berlin Lake in 1967. The United States Power Squadron helped to maintain a safe event. Various trophies were available.

EXHIBITS AND EXPOSITIONS. Scouts all over the world enjoy sharing what they do and what they know with others. The purpose of these public demonstrations of Scout skills are to educate and entertain. Boy Scout Exhibits and Expositions of all kinds have taken place throughout the years. They usually last two days over a week end.

The following are some of the public demonstrations that took place in our council at the Stambaugh Auditorium: 1921 Exhibit, 1936 Exposition, 1951 Exposition, 1959 Exhibit, and 1983 Exposition.

At the 1921 Exhibit, Governor Preus and Mayor Meyers attended.

The 1936 Exposition was a Merit Badge Show.

At the April 1951 Exposition, some 15,000 people visited. More than 1,000 Scouts, Cub Packs and Explorer Posts representing 53 booths participated in the show. The auditorium basement was jammed almost all the time during the two days the exposition ran. Mayor Charles P. Henderson, a member of the Boy Scout Council Executive Board, officially opened the Exposition at 7:00pm on Saturday following a short message of welcome. Robert A. Manchester, president of the Executive Committee, and M.M. Malmer, exposition chairman, also were on hand.

Scouts demonstrated everything from how to build bridges to mending a broken chair. From Chemistry to plumbing. They spliced ropes, made rope, made bows and arrows and showed how to shoot them. They explained boating, printed a newspaper, molded plaster and displayed a mammoth collection of live snakes, crawfish and frogs. A half gallon jar in the animal exhibition held what appeared to be a whole colony of garter snakes. In another exhibit, Sea Scouts rigged up a ship.

At the 1951 Exposition, Scouts revealed plans to erect a ten foot copper replica of the Statue of Liberty.

(1) G. Taylor Evans, Council President 1954-1956. (photo by Lee Banks, 1967). **(2)** 1917, first Executive Board, from left: Council Executive Conrad Meinecke, Mason Wick, Paul McLevey, W.W. Zimmerman, James L. Wick Jr., Harry Boyd, man in front unidentified. (A.D. Hamilton album). **(3)** 1988 Executive Board, from left, front row: Keith Downard, Bill Bresnahan, Council President Dr. David Ritchie, Council Executive Fred Baird, Council Commissioner Robert Davis, Tom Stabi. Middle row: Tony Valley Jr., Bill Shaper, Judge Fred Bailey, Viola Wayne, Michael Russell, Dr. Michael Wolocshak, Dave Diebel, Tom Malloy, Kevin Bokesch. Back row: Jim Parker, Jeff Dyer, Ed Susany, Richard Robart, Ron DiTosto. (photo by Jack Acri). **(4)** 1947, Eagle's cabin on the hill behind the Walker cabin, built in the 1920s by and for Eagle Scouts.

FFAMILY CAMP FOR SCOUT LEADERS. A modern up-to-date and completely equipped Scout Leader's Family Camp program was introduced in 1920 on Stambaugh Scout Reservation. Two separate articles indicated that it was situated in the area where the Baden Powell Cabin is today and where the old Oaks Campsite was located above the lake.

There was enough room for only three families each period on a first come, first serve basis.

Each tent was large with a fly and big porch in front. The equipment included one double cot and mattress, three single cots and mattresses, one hammock, one table, etc. Screening was provided as a protection from flies and mosquitoes. There was also a large kitchen and dining tent.

Every man that was in Scouting was entitled to all the privileges of this camp.

The purpose of this camp was to provide an ideal vacation for Scout leaders and their families, and at the same time to keep the largest number of leaders in touch with the Scout camp. Each man, while in camp, was asked to give four hours a day to the Boy Scout program, two hours in the morning and two in the afternoon. There were four periods of twelve days each.

The Hunter cabin, the Strouss cabin and Walker cabin were used by married members of the staff. These areas where off limits to campers and was then covered by heavy tree growth.

FARM HOUSE. There was an old farm house on the Stambaugh farm when the farm was given to the Scouts in 1919. It faced a yellow clay roadway that was in very poor condition named "Hell Road". The name was changed in 1921 to "Leffingwell Road" when improvements were made.

The large farm house had two floors and a basement. On the first floor, the east front room was the dining room with a door leading to the kitchen in the back. The bathroom was off of the kitchen. On the west side of the house was the living room running the length of the house with a door leading to the dining room. There was an old upright piano that sat in the front west corner of the living room.

An attached room located to the back west side of the living room became the workshop and office of the camp caretaker.

The stairs to the second floor were against the north wall of the living room. A long hallway went the length of the second floor from back to front. There were two bedrooms on either side of the hall with a storage room directly over the workshop. The master bedroom was on the north east side of the second floor.

The stairway to the basement was off the kitchen. A sink hand pump in the kitchen was used to get water. The water was warmed on an oil stove, even for the weekly bath. There was another hand pump for water outside behind the workshop.

The large house was heated by an old coal furnace located in the center of the basement. When it was cold outside, the first floor was cold like ice. All the heat would rise to the second floor. Of course there wasn't any insulation.

Harry Walker lived in the farm house with his family from 1922 until his retirement in 1945. He served as caretaker and camp director for the Stambaugh Scout Reservation.

In an interview with Harry Walker's daughter, Janet Walker Filban, she recalled her childhood in the farm house. She said Harry would play the mandolin and his wife would chord the old upright piano in the living room while the children sang songs.

She told me that one day during winter, Harry tried to fire up the coal furnace enough to heat the cold areas in the house. Harry's wife would tell him, "Don't fire that furnace too hot, your going to burn the house down". Janet remembers the smell of heated timbers in the basement due to the overheating.

On December 10, 1945, the first winter after the Walker family moved out of the farm house, it was destroyed by fire caused by someone overheating the coal furnace. The farm house was vacant. Camp Ranger Bob Kling and his family were to move into the house in the spring.

FIRE BELL. Prior to 1965, a large iron ring hung in front of the Katschke cabin. It was used as the camp fire warning system. Once the camp authorities were notified of a fire in camp, the iron ring was rung. It could be heard throughout the camp. A representative from each campsite and program area would report to the fire bell for further instruction.

On April 16, 1959, a 70 pound brass bell with mounting from an old railroad steam locomotive was presented to the safety division of St. John the Baptist School on Reed Avenue in Campbell. This bell served as an award for the school that entered a scrapbook showing the best school safety activities and with a school safety patrol. This was the first year for the award program. William L. Shorr of the Mahoning and Shenango Valley Railroad Community Committee made the presentation. The bell was awarded each year to the deserving school until 1963 when the award program ended. St. John the Baptist school won it that year also.

On December 12, 1964, Wesley Pollock, vice president of the school safety division presented the Stambaugh Scout Reservation with the 70 pound brass bell. This bell replaced the iron ring.

In August of 1965, Council Executive Henry Katschke built the brick altar and wood shelter to house the bell in the same location that the iron ring hung. The shelter for the brass bell was built over the original uprights and cross pole used for the iron ring. The bell, altar and shelter have remained the same since 1965.

One summer camp evening in 1967, Camp Director Bart Ingram and Camp Cook Bill Pusser were talking about having a surprise fire drill for the campers and staff. They were talking about it in private, so they thought! Nature Director Bill Kline and I overheard the conversation. We were typical teen-agers then who saw opportunity! So we decided to make a surprise of our own. We wrapped electrical tape around the gonger inside the bell. Just as the sun was setting Bill Pusser was directed by Bart Ingram to ring the bell. Bill rushes out the door of the Katschke cabin, he grabs the handle on the bell and begins swinging the bell back and forth with all his might. But to his surprise, the bell just went... thud, thud, thud!

Bill Kline and I had so much fun watching that event that our minds instantaneously created another surprise. After dark, we ran fishing line from where the Moyer Health Lodge was, through the trees, across the road to a tree that sat near the fire bell, down to the gonger inside the bell.

After the lights went out in the Katschke cabin, Bill and I pulled the fishing line a couple times and rang the bell from remote control. The porch light went on, the door opens and there stood our fearless leaders in their boxer shorts looking around. Not a pretty sight! But it sure was hilarious! The lights went out again and we rang the bell a second time. This time trousers went on the camp director and the cook and a search of the premises was made. But the fishing line was not detected. A third time the lights went out. We rang the bell again not immediately realizing that Bill Pusser was looking out the window!

I still wonder what thoughts went through his mind as he watched the "ghost of Stambaugh" ringing the bell. "Who did it?" has been a secret; until now!

Upon examination of the bell you will notice a nick on one side of the bell. During a summer camp season in the 1970s, an angered Scoutmaster, who displayed military accessories on a utility belt, went to the Katschke cabin, which served as the camp office, to see the camp director to make a complaint. When he didn't get the satisfaction he wanted, he pulled his machete out and hit the west side of the bell in anger. Now that's one way to leave your mark on camp! Military attire on Scouting is not permitted these days.

FIRST FEMALE REGISTERED. The first female member registered with the Boy Scouts of America on April 1, 1971. The Boy Scouts of America National Board approved female members in its Exploring program which was new at that time.

The first female member in our area was Karen Keeney at the age of 17. She registered in Explorer Post 248 which was a special interest organization that studied the history and lore of the American Indian.

FIRST SUMMER CAMP AT STAMBAUGH. The first official summer camp at the Stambaugh Scout Reservation opened July 4th, and closed August 30th in 1919. It was considered quite successful.

The aim and purpose of the camp that year was "to promote and develop the traits of character just awakening or perhaps still dormant in the boy. Life in the open was to instill in him a love for the great outdoors, associate him with companions of equal standards and provide a medium of exchange for experiences."

K.F. Miller was Camp Director. The camp committee at that time consisted of Lloyd R. Wallis as Chairman, W.W. Zimmerman, E.S. Brown, Harry A. Boyd, and Paul McKelvey.

The cost for board and transportation for a twelve day period was $8.95. Scouts brought their own provisions. Noon meals were made available for 25 cents. Any registered Scout in good standing in his troop and having the signed consent of his parents or guardian, and physician was allowed to attend camp. Boys expecting to attend camp could be examined free at the local Boy Scout headquarters.

There were four camp periods. The first one was July 7-19, second was July 21- August 2, the third was August 4-16, and the fourth was August 18-30.

Only 64 Scouts were allowed in camp each period. Absolutely no extension of the number was made. There was a waiting list in case of cancellations. A fee of $1.00 (one dollar) was required for registration deposit.

The tents at the camp were all double thick duck each with a fly. The sleeping tents were 14x16 feet and had floor boards. The dining and hospital tents were all tightly screened. All general table and kitchen ware were provided. The food was the best that could be obtained. The menu was under the doctor's charge and was "scientifically" arranged for the health of the campers. A first class cook with his right hand assistant prepared the meals.

There was a steel kitchen, the gift of the Truscon Steel Company. It was sanitary and modern in every way. Cool water from a drilled well made the Scouts forget that such a thing as thirst existed.

Visitors were welcome at the camp on Wednesday afternoon and evening and Sunday. However, those in charge of the camp suggested Sunday as the visiting day.

The following daily program was carried out:

6:55	am. First Call
7:00	Reveille
7:05	Setting up
7:15	Morning dip
7:25	Color raising
7:30	Breakfast
8:30	Sick and roll calls
9:00	Scoutcraft
10:00	Police grounds
10:30	Inspection and recreation
12:00	Noon dinner
1:00	pm. Rest period
2:00	Volunteer service
3:00	Scout games
4:00	Swimming and recreation
5:45	Parade, colors, etc.
6:00	Supper
7:00	Camp council and recreation
8:30	Camp fire
9:00	Tattoo
9:45	Taps

There were certain rules that were rigidly enforced. No firearms were allowed in the camp at any time and "sorry will be the lad who attempts to have them". A Scout is clean. Swimming was only permitted at specified swimming hours when instructors were in charge. Any infraction of this rule caused the Scout to be sent home and dismissed from the Scout movement. No one was allowed to leave camp without permission and the management kept a very close check on all the boys. The Scouts were discouraged from spending large sums of money.

Good clean fun, even at the other fellow's expense, was allowed. Pranks and tricks were allowed to be played if they stopped at the right time. Other jokes which could harm another were classed as a camp nuisance.

The athletic director was in charge of the Camp Field Day and conducted the examination for merit badges in his department. The Sabbath was a day of rest with religious services taking up a few hours. Sunday school groups convened at 10:00 am. There were carpenters benches and tools for the boys interested in this line of work. All Scouts were required to perform stunts around the campfire.

Scouts who expected to attend camp for any period were required to have all bad teeth fixed before camp and they had to have their hair cut short. The boys were required to wear their night shirts and pajamas.

There was a small store where wholesome candy could be bought. Films, stamps and postal cards were also sold. The boys were required to write home at least once a week to let their folks know how they were getting along.

All camp labor was done by paid help. Scouts were required to do some small duties such as guard duty and waiting on tables.

FLAG DAY. On Flag Day every year before 1952, Scouts gathered at Wick Park for flag ceremonies where the public was invited. In 1951, The Boy Scouts decided that decentralized flag ceremonies might interest a larger number of people. From that time on troops held flag raising and retreat in their own neighborhoods which roused wide public interest.

On June 10, 1954, Council Executive Henry Katschke, Council President G. Taylor Evans and other council officials were on a television show at an Akron station to receive the Freedom Foundation Award for the council's Flag Day participation in 1953.

On Monday June 15, 1959, Scouts conducted special flag raising and retreat ceremonies throughout the valley for the 25th Flag Day.

In the April 1965 edition of Scouting Magazine on pages 12 and 13, is a page and a half article written by Council Executive Henry Katschke titled, "Flag Day At Mahoning Valley". It explains the tradition of decentralized flag ceremonies.

FLAG POLE. About fifty feet into the woods off of Leffingwell Road across from the horse farm drive way is the remains of a cement base with a large rusted off metal flag pole in it. On the cement base is inscribed "1941".

FORDYCE, GEORGE L. Fordyce was council president in 1913. He owned the George L. Fordyce Company in downtown Youngstown which was located at W. Federal and south Phelps streets. He was one of the countries leading naturalists and bird experts and was president of the Youngstown City Hospital Association.

FUND CAMPAIGN OF 1915. A campaign was conducted for funds to care for a three year budget. A member of the National Staff, J.P. Freeman, was secured to carry on the drive.

(1) Remains of the Stambaugh farm house after it burned down December 10, 1945. The red hay barn is in the background, garage is at left. **(2)** George L. Fordyce, first Council President in 1913. (Mahoning Valley Historical Society). **(3-4)** Camp fire alarm. **(3)** Prior to 1965, this large iron ring was used. **(4)** In 1965, a railroad locomotive bell replaced the iron ring. (photos 3,4 by Henry Katschke).

GAS PUMP IN CAMP. A manually operated gasoline pump was used in camp prior to the 1970s. Using a lever, gas was hand pumped up to a glass container that was located on top of the pump. After the amount of gas needed was in the top chamber, it was fed by gravity through a hose into the camp vehicle.

Later it was replaced by a submergible electric pump. Abuse by volunteers caused its removal.

GATEWAY STONE PILLARS INTO CAMP. These pillars were originally built in 1930 by Troop 15. The cement used in its construction was donated by Bessemer Cement Company in Pennsylvania.

Sometime in the 1970s, Don Baumgartner and Henry McNatt made repairs to the stone pillar gateway. Some of the stones and mortar had broken loose over the years.

Then in 1992, a delivery truck ran into the west pillar breaking the top part off. It was repaired.

Rumor has it that behind the face plate on the east pillar is a glass bottle time capsule dating back to 1930 with memorabilia sealed in it.

GRANGER, KARL. Mr. Granger was Scoutmaster of Troop 44 for about ten years in Poland during the 1940s. He loved being Scoutmaster and teaching his Scouts about nature. He also loved his horse "Rocky".

Karl Granger's Scouts of yesteryear still remember him riding his horse proudly through the Poland woods. Legend has it that after the horse died, Mr. Granger buried his horse in the Poland woods. A large rock marks its grave.

GREEN, ROY H. Roy Green was an active leader in the Boy Scout program and a naturalist who instructed nature study in camp. The birds and animals would come to his hand to feed. In a 1930s black and white 16mm movie film taken on the Stambaugh Scout Reservation, it shows Roy Green and his animals.

He made and maintained a wild flower garden in camp in the early 1930s. The garden was near the approach to the council fire ring. After his death at age 61 on October 27, 1935, the garden deteriorated.

As a tribute to Roy Green, a tombstone shaped rock was laid near the council fire ring among the wild flowers. The stone read: "Roy Green, 1935".

In the 1970s, Camp Ranger Don Mikkelson cleared an area for a garden to the approach of the council ring for the natural wild flowers. Don named this area "Nature's Garden". He placed Roy Green's stone in Nature's Garden.

Green died from a six foot fall down a flight of steps at the William B. Pollock Company where he worked as watchman for 35 years. He was buried at Forest Lawn Memorial Cemetery.

Roy Green was born in Rushford, New York June 21, 1874. He was married with two children.

"GREEN BAR BILL", WILLIAM HILLCOURT. He was born in Denmark on August 6, 1900. He immigrated to the United States in 1926 and joined the National staff of the Boy Scouts of America that same year. After retiring in 1965, he wrote many remarkable books on nature and conservation as well as the best known biography of Scouting's founder, titled: "Baden Powell: The Two Lives Of A Hero". William Hillcourt was personal friends with Mr. and Mrs. Baden Powell.

He was a program specialist for the Boy Scouts of America and was our first deputy camp chief and first Wood Badge course director in the United States. He was also the National Director of Scoutcraft and assistant editor of "Boys Life Magazine".

He was the author of the first American "Handbook For Patrol Leaders" (1929), the "Handbook For Scoutmasters" (1960), and the "Official Boy Scout Handbook" 1979.

He also authored earlier editions of the "Fieldbook" and "Outdoor Things To Do".

He received his Wood Badge beads in 1939. Whenever a Wood Badger serves on a Wood Badge staff, the Wood Badger is given a third bead. William Hillcourt's third bead was from the long necklace of wooden beads captured by Baden Powell from Chief Dinizulu.

In 1948 he developed and directed as Scoutmaster, Wood Badge Course #1 in the United States. This was the first Wood Badge course ever attempted in America. This course took place at Schiff Scout Reservation in New Jersey July 31-August 8.

In August of 1989, William Hillcourt was guest for two days in Camp Stambaugh at our council's first Boy Scout Wood Badge Training Course BC-390. I enjoyed talking with Bill Hillcourt and listening to his stories. He was personal friends with Baden Powell, James E. West and other early day pioneers of Scouting.

"Green Bar Bill" Hillcourt died on November 9, 1992 at age 92 in Stockholm after completing a tour of Japan as a guest of the Boy Scouts of Nippon and Russia.

(1) View from K.L. Brown Pavilion toward ranger's home and gatehouse (right). (photo by Henry Katschke, 1949). (2) Stone pillar at entrance to Camp Stambaugh in 1931. (16mm movie film frame. (3) Roy Green, 1935. (Youngstown Historical Society).

HAM RADIO IN CAMP STAMBAUGH. During the 1970s and early 1980s, a large antenna could be seen at the top of a tall tower connected to the side of the gatehouse near the entrance into camp. This was where Ham Radio Operator Attorney Richard Shelar operated his radio. He was able to transmit and receive from all over the world.

Radio Merit Badge and FCC Novice Amateur license classes were held weekly by Shelar in camp.

For several years during the 1970s, Camp Stambaugh Ham Radio Station W8CCV/8 was on the air participating in the "Boy Scout Jamboree On The Air". Scout stations around the world transmitted in code and voice communicating with each other. On one occasion I know of on October 16, 1977, President Carter sent greetings over the air waves.

I remember some of the fun nights on the radio with Shelar, along with a large pizza with everything and plenty of Pepsi.

HAMILTON, A.D. He was a longtime Scouting leader and friend to all. His service spans over 48 years in Mahoning Valley Council.

Aubrey D. Hamilton was born June 21, 1892, in Youngstown. He married in 1913 and had two sons.

It was in 1930 that he began his Scouting career when he became Scoutmaster of Troop 34. He received the Silver Beaver award in 1949 and was well known for his historical knowledge of the development of Camp Stambaugh.

A.D. (as he was called) was instrumental in organizing the O.A. lodge in its beginning. He became a Vigil Honor Arrowman in the Order of the Arrow

After his death at age 85 in May 1978, the Order of the Arrow "A.D. Hamilton Memorial Campership Fund" was established to recognize his service to youth.

HANDBOOK FOR BOYS. The first "Americanized" handbook of the Boy Scouts was printed in 1911.

HANDICAPPED CHILDREN. The first summer camping session was held for physically and mentally handicapped children in 1984.

HARDING'S FUNERAL. In August of 1923, a selected group of 16 Scouts and leaders under the leadership of S.S. French, an executive board member, and Chief Meinecke represented the Youngstown Council at the funeral of President Warren G. Harding.

Harding was honorary president of the Boy Scouts of America. The local delegation was one of many groups from cities through the state, all assisting the National Guard in caring for the crowds.

HARRER, DR. J. GEORGE. He was the 6th Eagle Scout in the council. He became president of the Rockerfeller Foundation.

HERBERT HOOVER AWARD. This was a ten year growth program adopted by National in 1930.

Herbert Hoover offered this award to each troop that reached certain standards. Forty-one local troops received the award at the largest Scout meeting ever held to date. The Drum and Bugle Corp was present with W.H. Cook presiding.

HIK-O-REE AT MILL CREEK PARK. The "Mill Creek Park Adventure Hik-O-Ree" was held in the fall of 1975 by the Outriders under the boy leadership of Ralph Siegrist and adult advisors Tony Valley Jr, Joe Angelo Sr, and Nick Valley.

Troops hiked and Cubs biked around Mill Creek Park stopping at stations along the way, instead of the usual weekend fall camporee. The stations were designed to be educational rather than competitive.

Those participating in the stations were: Ohio Edison with a film and narration on pollution and energy, Gold Cross with ambulance display and emergency services, Red Cross with emergency services, R.E.A.C.T. C.B. radio operation, Mahoning Valley Colonial Brigade with Men of Bicentennial display and firing of old time rifles, and the United States Marine Corp with defense of our country, amphibious vehicles and weapons, Mayor Hunter of Youngstown as guest speaker at the closing rally and WFMJ Channel 21.

About 125 Boy Scouts and 85 Cub Scouts plus leaders and staff attended. A 5½" square full color patch was available.

HONOR MEDAL RECEIVED BY LOCAL BOY. In 1919 the National Court of Honor granted an Honor Medal to Eagle Scout Charles Higby of Troop 9. He had been stricken with infantile paralysis. He received the award for rendering heroic service in contributing his blood to the relief of another victim of the same disease.

HOOVER CABIN. In the late 1920s, the Sheet & Tube Steel Company had labor camps for its workers. These were located on Mt. Vernon Street near Walton Street in Struthers. There were simple buildings made of wooden frames and tree slabs lined in rows for the mill workers to stay in.

Earl Timblin, Scoutmaster of Troop 54 at that time, was given one of those wooden buildings for Stambaugh. That wooden building and a corn shed that existed on the Stambaugh farm was used to build the Hoover Cabin by Troop 54 in 1929. A stone built into the fireplace reads: "Troop 54 BSA, Third Reformed Church, Erected MCMXXIX".

The cabin was named after the 31st President of the United States, Herbert Hoover, who was president at that time.

Troop 54 was the first Troop to camp in the Hoover cabin. It was their cabin and they took care of the cabin maintenance. Later, other troops were permitted to use the cabin.

In 1950, the Sheet & Tube Company donated blankets, cooking utensils, dishes and silverware to be used in the Hoover cabin.

Troop 54 was chartered 1927 by the Third Reformed Church on Midlothian at Sheridan. The church later changed its name to Bethlehem United Church of Christ.

In 1949, the back porch was enclosed and used as a kitchen. It had a wood burner stove.

In 1951, the inside of the Hoover cabin was refinished in yellow pine. The roofed porch that ran the whole length of the south side of the cabin that existed since the cabin's beginning in 1929, was now decayed and replaced with a smaller porch.

Renovating the Hoover cabin was a must on the renovation and reconditioning program of 1955. Volunteer brick masons interested in Scouting repaired the fire place that was in poor condition. It would leak smoke into the cabin whenever a fire was built in the fire place. The outside walls were recovered to protect the cabin from the weather and make it more presentable.

The Hoover cabin accommodated 24 Scouts and leaders on almost every week end. Because it was one of Stambaugh's larger cabins, it was always in great demand.

In 1973, Troop 54 removed the weather beaten outer finish of the cabin once again and with the help of the C.B.'s put a new finish on the cabin.

Later, the enclosed back porch was opened as it was originally.

My troop, #7, did plenty of camping in the Hoover cabin. While I was a Scout, my Scoutmaster, Mr. Larry Drombetta, designated me to be the troop bugler since

I was a trumpet player.

On one winter campout in the mid 1960s we were camping in the Hoover cabin. It was 10:00 pm. The cabin lights were out and Scouts were silent. Only the crackling of the fire in the fire place could be heard. The fire's glow was dancing on the ceiling.

I played my usual taps standing in front of the fireplace silhouetted only by the fire light. Everything was as it always was that evening as our day came to an end, except I decided to play my trumpet instead of the bugle.

Hanging from my little left finger was a lid from one of the troop cook kit pots. On a pre-arranged plan, when I just about reached the end of taps, I dropped the lid to the floor intentionally as a signal. Upon the signal, my fellow troop members began turning lights on and off, banging pots and metal bunk frames while I played a vigorous "Hurray for the red, white and blue". We thought it was hilarious. But a difference in opinion seemed to exist between us in our teen years and our Scoutmaster. Needless to say, my Scoutmaster was not happy. I know that for a fact because he sent me outside into the cold snow and told me to play taps over and over again until my lips fall off!

HUNTER, HARRY. Hunter came to Youngstown from Louisville, Kentucky and was hired as council executive on October 29, 1923. He left Youngstown in April of 1936 to be council executive in Harrisburg, Pennsylvania. After he retired, he returned to Youngstown and in 1956 became lodge advisor to the Order of the Arrow. He was a guiding hand in the 1957 reorganization of our lodge.

HUNTER CABIN. The Hunter cabin was built in 1931 by the Men's Club and boys of Troop 36 of St. John's Episcopal Church. It was named in honor of Council Executive Harry H. Hunter. Hunter and his family occasionally lived in this cabin during the summer camping season.

William Henry Cook raised the money to build the cabin. He also designed and supervised its construction.

Through the 1930s and most of the 1940s, the cabin was the home of Troop 36. They kept the cabin in repair.

During the summer camp season from the cabin's beginning, part of the cabin was used as a trading post and post office.

During summer camp through the late 1940s and the 1950s, the Hunter cabin also served as camp headquarters. On off season weekends, troops camped in the cabin.

From 1986 to 1992, the Order of the Arrow began using the Hunter cabin as their own. The O.A. used the cabin to hold their lodge meetings, store ceremonial equipment, costumes, and display O.A. memorabilia that was available for the campers to see. They also became responsible for operating the trading post during weekends in the off season. The Trading Post was in a separate room of the Hunter cabin. During summer camp, the Trading Post was in the charge of the camp director and business manager and the O.A. meeting room was used for leaders meetings.

(1) Harry Hunter, Council Executive, 1923-1936. **(2)** Marty Wendt (left) and A.D. Hamilton, 1963. **(3)** Hunter cabin (Trading Post), circa 1931. (Ed Cook album). **(4)** Hoover cabin, 1954. (photo by Spratt Studio).

I INCOME. In the early days of the council, income was dependent on council membership dues.

In 1915, a campaign was conducted for funds to care for a three-year budget. A member of the National Staff, J.P. Freeman, was secured to carry on the drive.

Before the Community Chest, the Rotary Club raised $15,000 for the council in 1916.

Another means to raise money beginning in 1916 was an Indian show in Mill Creek Park using real Indians.

INDIAN LAKE. When Camp Stambaugh began its first summer camp season in 1919, Indian Lake did not exist. There was only a pure clear stream of water known as "Indian Creek" that ran through the property.

In 1920, Indian Creek was widened to make a small mud pond at one point just east of the Chief's Cabin. A temporary earthen dam was built from the dirt and rock that came from the pond. The pond quickly grew muddy when used and sometimes the earthen dam was entirely washed away.

By July of 1922, Scout membership was at 1,100 in Youngstown. To accommodate the increase in use of the mud pond, Harry Walker enlarged the pond by using a horse drawn wooden scoop. Dirt and stone from the pond was used to make the first solid mud and rock wall dam. The dam was four feet tall making the water neck deep for most of the Scouts. That year the lake became known as "Lake-up-to-my-neck-ee" after Council Executive Conrad Meinecke (my-neckee). The horse that pulled the scoop was named Barney. Barney lived in the stable under the red barn (known today as the K.L. Brown Pavilion).

When the Scouts were in the mud pond, a whistle was blown every ten minutes for Scouts and their buddies to line up on shore for a buddy check and a game. H.H. Biggs of the National Red Cross Life Saving Corps was swimming director.

In the spring of 1923, a 4-acre artificial lake and dam of stone, cement, and railroad ties was made. The lake was named "Indian Lake" because it is part of Indian Creek. The dam had stone and cement supports with railroad ties laid across them. This was part of a special improvement program for which campaign funds were collected.

In 1930, a diving platform was built to the right of the Pioneer cabin so Scouts who were very good swimmers could dive into the deepest part of the lake.

In the years to follow, flooding from heavy rain caused damage.

In the early 1930s, heavy rain caused the lake to flood washing away part of the dam.

In 1945, the original stone and cement dam that was built in 1923, was made higher by building cement pillars on top of the existing structure. This made the lake deeper which brought the water level up to the foundation of the Chief's Cabin on the north shore of the lake.

A flood in the early spring of 1947 and again in 1952 washed out the railroad ties from the south gate of the dam.

In 1953, concrete reinforcement jackets were constructed around the existing upright structures of the dam and side walls. Vertical I-beams were installed to support and channel horizontal railroad ties that held back the water. The channels also made raising and lowering the ties easier with the use of a portable hand operated winch

As part of the Camp Stambaugh capital improvement project of May 1955, a boat dock was built in front of the Pioneer cabin, a new 60 foot swimming pier replaced the old one, a cement floor replaced the wooden floor of the non-swimmers crib and a new fence was built around the lake. All wood projects were made of white oak.

Then, in the early morning of May 12, 1956, one of the worst flooding disasters at Camp Stambaugh happened. A heavy rain storm washed away a 40 foot section of the earthen dam and the rushing water flooded the assembly field as high as the dining hall and other areas adjacent to Indian Creek. The new boat dock built in 1955 near the Chief's Cabin was washed against the dam. Water undermined the foundation of the dining hall and the foundation of the bridge over the creek that is located below the dam. The roads in camp had two foot gullies from running water. This happened just before the spring camporall where 1,500 Scouts were to show up and before summer camp was to open. Damages caused by the heavy rain, wind and high water were in excess of $10,000. Substantial contributions from various individuals were immediately received. The camp did not have insurance for water and flood damage. The dam and other repairs were made as rapidly as possible. They were completed by June 24th when summer camp began. Seven-hundred Scouts were enrolled for camp in 1956.

Despite the damages, the annual camporall was held the week-end following the flood with conservation specialists working with Scouts on various phases of conservation to repair the camp.

During the 1961 and 1962 summer camp season, the health department was close to closing the lake because of a high bacteria count.

Camp Ranger Don Mikkelson recalls taking daily water samples from Indian Lake to the health department so they could monitor the bacteria level.

To help alleviate the problem without closing the lake, a clorination system to clorinate Indian Lake was installed and used in 1961 and 1962. A small building was built near the lake to house the clorinator and pump.

More heavy rains during summer camp August 8, 1970, caused the lake to overflow its banks once again. Camp staff and volunteer Scouters made sand bags and laid them along the banks of the lake and creek to contain the rushing water. The cause of the flooding was due to a break in a temporary earthen dam up-creek just west of Raccoon Road. This dam was used while route 11 was being built. Tons of silt was dumped into Indian Lake as a result of the route 11 dam breaking. We were unable to use the lake for motorboating and sailing.

Early in the morning of the flood, the kitchen steward was walking to the dining hall, as he did every morning, when he heard rushing water near the lake. It sounded different than usual. As he looked, water was flooding over the earth part of the dam and running into the assembly field. He hurriedly ran to wake up Camp Director Bart Ingram. Gently shaking Bart's shoulder the steward said, "Mr. Ingram, wake up. Water is running over the dam". Bart's eyes opened, he looked at the steward and said, "water is supposed to run over the dam"! The steward replied, "All the way to the dining hall"?

Camp Director Bart Ingram made several attempts at contacting the Ohio Department of Highways for their assistance in this matter but with little result.

As the years passed, the council made several attempts on their own to clean the silt out of Indian Lake, but the heavy equipment just sank into the bottom of the lake making it impossible to move.

If the lake could have remained drained for at least one full year it probably would have dried out enough to allow equipment on the lake bed without sinking. But a drained lake in the summer meant no boating program.

Then in the winter of 1985/1986, three local heavy equipment operators, Jim Brown, Bob Brown, and Jack

Mahley from Grim's Crane Service in East Palestine Ohio donated their time and equipment to start cleaning out the lake. They dredged Indian Lake from the bank by swinging a huge bucket on a long boom into the lake bed. Silt four feet deep was removed from part of the lake and was dropped on the east side of the earthen dam to dry. A year later the dry dirt was leveled. Further progress was halted when the owner of the crane service passed away.

INDIAN PAGEANT IN MILL CREEK PARK. In 1915 and 1916, Troop 23 from Richard Brown Memorial Church at Elm Street and Woodbine Avenue brought the Hiawatha Indian Company to Mill Creek Park to perform the "Hiawatha Indian Pageant". Genuine Iroqouis Indians from upper New York State performed during the two week pageant.

The pageant took place for two weeks on the flats near the lake. The Indians made Tee-Pees to sleep in and birch bark canoes to travel up and down the lake in.

Troop 23 used the pageant to raise money for camping equipment.

For several weeks during the month of June in 1948, another Indian Pageant was performed west of Lake Newport in Mill Creek Park. This time several hundred Boy Scouts and Cub Scouts from our council performed. Wearing war paint and dressed in authentic costumes of many Indian tribes, the Scouts performed a pageant based on Kenneth Robert's novel of pre-Revolutionary War days, "Northwest Passage".

INNER CITY SCOUTING. Inner City Scouting began in the late 1960s.

The following companies donated equipment and money for this program: Sears Roebuck & Company, Penn-Ohio Towel Supply Company, and General Electric Lamp Division.

(1) Scouts learning a lifesaving technique at the swimming hole in Indian Creek, 1922. Wood planks reinforced the mud and stone dam in background. (Robert Manchester album). **(2)** Early 1930s, Harry Walker (left) and cousin Will Rogers, use wood and tar-paper to increase dam height two feet. (Vindicator/Frondorf album). **(3 & 4)** May 12, 1956. The worst flood ever in Camp Stambaugh. **(3)** Eroded 40 foot section of the earthen dam. **(4)** Bridge below the dam. **(5)** The dam after high water washed railroad ties away from one of the gates in 1952. Note original stone and cement dam support built in 1923 under the cement pillar addition that was built in 1945. (photos 3,4,5 by Spratt Studio). **(6)** Early 1940s, Wick Lodge in background. (16mm movie film).

(1) Two lakefront instructors below Indian Lake dam in 1935. Tent tops and flagpole (left) is the Sea Lion Stockade campsite. Pioneer cabin and diving platform is to the right. (2) Swimming pier, 1956. Non-swimmer crib (left) and beginner area is inside pier. (3) Scouts swimming in Indian Lake, 1932. (photo by Ed Cook). (4) Bart Ingram, Camp Director, 1967-1971. (photo by author, 1985). (5) Diving platform on the north side of the lake near the Chief's cabin where only Scouts qualified as swimmer were permitted. (16mm movie film). (6) The Sea Lion Stockade campsite (in background), 1935 on the south shore of Indian Lake, west of the Wick Lodge. Aquatic, health and athletic programs were taught here. Sea Lions cooked and ate in the pavilion at upper left. (7) Chief's cabin (Pioneer cabin) on north shore of Indian Lake, west of dam. (photos 1,6 by Milton Revzin; photos 2,7 by Spratt Studio).

J **JAMBOREE AT VALLEY FORGE, 1950.** Sixty-two Scouts had a practice week-end at Camp Stambaugh in June for the National Jamboree at Valley Forge in Pennsylvania. An article in the Vindicator read: "The hottest thing at the Boy Scout's National Jamboree beyond a doubt is the shoe leather".

About 47,000 Scouts and their leaders camped on the historic site where Washington's army stayed in the winter of 1777. Scouts were there from the United States as well as some of the U.S. territories and 19 other nations.

Our council delegation was lead by Al Hughes, assistant executive of our council; George Woodman, Scoutmaster of the First Presbyterian Church Troop 9; J.E. Bowers of Hubbard Scoutmaster of Coalburg Troop 112; and Reverend L.C. Pretty of Hubbard, pastor of Hubbard Lutheran Church.

Our Scouts left for Valley Forge aboard a special train that was made up on the Baltimore & Ohio railroad. They assembled at Scout headquarters on E. Rayen Avenue in Youngstown on a Tuesday evening and marched to the train boarding station at 8:00 pm. A delegation from Warren joined them at the train station.

The train made frequent stops on its eastward trip to pick up other units. The train arrived at Valley Forge on Wednesday.

Scouts camped on a 625-acre section of Valley Forge Park. The jamboree grounds were divided into 1,292 sectional camp sites each of which accommodated 34 troops. Each troop had 35 Scouts or Explorers and three adult leaders. Each section had its own service tent, post office, health lodge, and shower facilities.

The jamboree climaxed the 40th anniversary of the Boy Scouts of America and was part of their crusade "to strengthen the arm of liberty".

The Scouts did their own cooking over charcoal fires and ate on paper plates. President Truman, honorary president of the Scouts, opened the jamboree June 30, 1950. A pageant telling the story of Washington at Valley Forge was performed as well as exhibits and demonstrations of Scoutcraft.

Scouts toured Philadelphia, some 24 miles to the east of the Jamboree. They traveled into the city by bus. They saw Independence Hall and the Betsy Ross house among other historic sites.

Youngstown Scouts went to Washington D.C. for an eight-hour site seeing trip. They arrived back in town July 9th.

JAMBOREE AT MORAINE STATE PARK, 1973. On August 3-9, 1973, 40,000 Scouts and 4,000 leaders from 50 states and 50 countries attended the National Jamboree East in Pennsylvania. This was the first year that the Jamboree was held in two locations. Jamboree West was held at Farragut Park in Idaho, August 1-7. Wayne Stoyer was chairman of the council jamboree committee. Some 250 Youngstown area Scouts and leaders attended.

JOHNSON, M. DEAN. Dean was Council Executive of Mahoning Valley Council from June 1968 to September 1974. Do to ill health, he resigned to accept the position of Finance Director with the Philadelphia Council. He died February 19, 1975.

Dean came from a Scouting family. His father was Council Executive for several councils and also served on the Regional and National Staff. Dean started Scouting as a boy and attained the rank of Eagle Scout. During his 17 years of professional Scouting before coming to Youngstown, he was Field Executive for Tomahawk Council in Coshocton Ohio, and later served at Marion Ohio, Louisville Kentucky, and Assistant Council Executive of the Greater Cleveland Council.

He served as camp director and was on the staff of many camp schools, Jamborees, National training events and at Schiff Reservation in New Jersey.

Dean was married to Barbara and had three sons, Matt, Jeff, and David.

At the 1973 National Jamboree at Moraine State Park in Pennsylvania. **(1)** Troop 7 from St. Anthony's. Sitting from left: Bill Huey, Vince Altieri, Hoffman, Dom Salomone, Dom Valley, Jesse Salomone, Hoffman, Hoffman. Leaders are (A) Scoutmaster Henry Sforza and (B) Tony Valley Jr. **(2)** Troop 38 from Pleasant Grove Presbyterian Church, from left: John Kramer, Claud Vasu, Chuck Petzinger, John VanDyke, Scoutmaster Emil Rauschenbach (age 73), Brad Kibbel, Jerry Burkholder, Rick Zenn, John Shaw and Anthony Bettile. (photos 1,2 by Vindicator). **(3)** M. Dean Johnson, Council Executive from 1968-1974. (photo by Lee Banks).

KATSCHKE, HENRY E. Katschke was Council Executive for Mahoning Valley Council from June 1, 1949 - February 29, 1968. He served the longest term as Council Executive in Mahoning Valley Council.

Katschke was born September 7, 1903 in Toledo. He became a Scout in 1918 and attained the rank of First Class Scout and later was a Scoutmaster and volunteer leader. In 1926 he became field executive for Toledo Council. In 1932, he went to Coshocton as a Council Executive and in 1936 was transferred to Mountaineer Area Council in Fairmont West Virginia. On September 15, 1940 he went to the Tri-State Area Council in Huntington West Virginia.

On June 1, 1949 he came to Youngstown as Council Executive, succeeding Kenneth L. Brown who retired.

The Scouting program in Youngstown more than doubled under Katschke's leadership. In 1949 the council had an annual budget of $41,000 and an enrollment of 2,625 in Cub Scout, Boy Scout and Explorer programs. In 1967, the council spent $125,000 and had an enrollment of 6,000 boys. There were seven full time council staff with 2,400 volunteer adult leaders.

Katschke received his Vigil Honor in the Order of the Arrow in our council on September 1, 1962 with the Indian name, "Sakima", meaning "Chief".

Katschke's professional career followed a desire to repay a favor to Scouting. He said, "Until Scouting came along, I was on my way to becoming a juvenile delinquent. I promised myself that if I ever had the chance I would repay the Scouting movement for what it did for me".

Katschke authored two published articles. One in the April 1965 issue of "Scouting Magazine" on page 12 & 13 titled, "Flag Day At Mahoning Valley", and the other in "Now And Then", a newsletter for retired Scouting professionals on page 2 titled, "My Hobby Building Creches".

Katschke retired March 1, 1968 ending 50 years of Scouting with 42 of those years as a professional Scouter.

Katschke wrote in his close-out report, "Working these past years in the Mahoning Valley Council has proved to me the statement, 'He who says traditions are useless, is like a leaf saying the roots of a tree are useless".

Henry and his wife Verda had two sons, both Eagle Scouts.

Henry E. Katschke died in May, 1971.

KATSCHKE LODGE. This cabin was originally built in the early 1930s and was named "Chief's Lodge".

From the early 1930s up to 1949, an open porch and the entrance into the cabin was on the east side of the building toward where the Spruce Triangle is today. A dirt road to the bottom of the camp ran only in the front of the cabin and then curved toward the Meinecke Lodge (dining hall). Trees and undergrowth were all around the cabin. A natural spring water fountain was on the north side of the cabin.

In 1949, Henry Katschke was hired as Council Executive. He began to hold many council organizational meetings in this cabin.

Because Katschke was Chief of the council, this cabin became known as "Chief's Lodge".

Camp committee chairman Walter Chuck told the camp committee that the council executive needed a place in camp to meet with committees, leaders, and individual Scouters to plan the Scouting program. So, the camp committee gave approval to enlarging the cabin by enclosing the porch that was on the east side of the cabin and placing a new entrance on the south side of the enclosed section of the porch. Flush toilet facilities and running water were added onto the back of the cabin.

Katschke renamed the cabin "Katschke Lodge". He remodeled the inside with knotty pine wood. Back in those days pianos were shipped in wooden crates made of knotty pine wood. So Henry would go down town to a piano store and collect the discarded wood.

During the summer months that followed, the camp director lived in the lodge. Special guests visiting the camp would sometimes stay there.

After Henry Katschke retired February 29, 1968, the camp committee passed a motion on May 14, 1968 to have Henry Katschke's cabin officially named the "Katschke Lodge". The council executive board approved it July 1, 1968.

Some Scouters rebelled and demanded the name be changed back to "Chief's Lodge".

Today the cabin is used solely during summer camp as the camp office.

In 1993, the rest room attached to the back of the cabin was replaced with a new rest room and shower facility in order to accommodate female leaders.

KNIGHTS OF DUNAMIS. The first chapter of the Knights of Dunamis started in 1919 in the San Francisco Council. This organization was a National Honor Fraternity consisting of only Eagle Scouts. Their purpose was to help strengthen the advancement program in units and provide special counseling and service to new leaders. They also performed memorable courts of honor for new Eagle Scouts.

By 1957, Eagles in Youngstown wanted a chapter of their own. Lou Flickenger was very much in support of this program and volunteered to become advisor. Our chapter operated until the 1970s when National phased out the program.

One year, twenty-one Eagle Scouts from our council attended inaugural festivities in Washington D.C.

Then in April of 1974, twelve Eagle Scouts and advisor Ray Slaven attended the Cherry Blossom festival in Washington D.C. Professional staff advisor was District Executive Dave McCalla.

There was a brief period of time when the adult Eagles in our council tried to take over the program, but the council remained firm to maintain the Knights of Dunamis as a youth operated program.

(1) Henry E. Katschke, 1949. Council Executive, 1949-1968. (2-6) Katschke Lodge. (2) Built in the early 1930s and originally named Chief's Lodge. It had an open porch on the east side. (3) Front of Katschke Lodge in 1949 after the porch was enclosed. (4-5) Inside, 1951. (photos 3,4,5 by Henry Katschke), (photos 1,2, Henry Katschke album). (6) Lodge in 1985. (7) Framed painting symbolizing Henry Katshcke's activities and beliefs. (photos 6,7 by author).

Dedicated to the memory of
Henry E. Katschke
Scout Executive, Mahoning
Valley Council, 1949-1968

L **LOG RUN.** Behind the chapel on the hill at the north side of the creek in the 1940s, many years before the chapel existed, logs were slid down a wooden trough that sat in a gully. The gully can still be seen today.

LONE SCOUTS OF AMERICA. The original Lone Scouts idea began in England in 1913 and was designed for isolated rural boys.

The Lone Scouts of America operated from 1915 to 1924 and enrolled more than a half-million boys. Chicago publisher William D. Boyce started it in America. Boyce helped to incorporate the Boy Scouts of America on February 8, 1910.

By the end of 1914, the Boy Scouts of America had a membership of 275,000 boys and men, most of them in cities and towns. Millions of boys who lived in far rural areas had little chance of belonging to a troop because of the distance.

Boyce's plan for organizing the LSA (Lone Scouts of America) was to bring Scouting to those boys in the rural areas through his magazine titled "Lone Scout". The first issue was published October 30, 1915 and cost one cent which was the only membership fee for the Lone Scouts at that time. Five years later, Lone Scout Magazine went to monthly publication and cost 10 cents a copy. Every cover featured an American Indian drawn by Perry Emerson Thompson. The Indian theme was used throughout the magazine. Boyce was titled Chief Totem and the Chicago headquarters became the Long House. Boys joining formed tribes headed by a Chief.

Like Boy Scouting, Lone Scouting had its ranks, called degrees. There were seven degrees in three "lodges", (1) Tepee, (2) Totem Pole, and (3) Sagamore. Five badges could be earned within the lodges. The highest title was Supreme Scout.

Lone Scouts had no adult leaders. They were on their honor when they wrote to headquarters to report that they had passed tests.

There was a uniform for those who could afford one. It was a Norfolk jacket, knickers, puttees, and hat. The uniform then cost around $12 including canteen and knapsack.

Relations between the LSA and BSA officials remained limited.

The year after Lone Scouting began, the BSA started its own program called "Pioneers" specifically for rural boys. It used the regular Boy Scout advancement plan with an adult as guide and test examiner. The Pioneer program was not very successful.

The Lone Scouts of America merged with the Boy Scouts of America on March 1, 1924. Chief Scout Executive James E. West reported a conservative Lone Scout membership at that time at 45,000. The BSA published its own magazine for rural boys until 1956 titled "The Lone Scout".

(1) Ross Lucarell, Camp Ranger, 1983 to present. (photo by author, 1985). (2) May 1920 cover of the "Lone Scout" magazine. (Scouting Magazine, October 1985). (3) 1950s latrine. (4) One of the washing and latrine facilities placed in campsites as part of the Long Range Plan of 1962, camp improvement projects. (photos 3,4 by Lee Banks).

47

MAHONING COUNTY HISTORICAL BIKE ROUTE. The Mahoning County Historical Bike Route was designed by Robert B. Conklin of Troop 46 in 1977 as an Eagle Scout project and was sponsored by the Order of the Arrow, Neatoka Lodge #396.

The route is about 38 miles long and follows hard surface roads throughout the county passing through fifteen historical points of interest.

The route starts at Boardman Park. It travels through Mill Creek Park and works it way to Canfield and on to Camp Stambaugh. Then it travels through New Middletown, and Poland returning to Boardman Park.

Some points of interest are: St. James Church in Boardman Park, the Old Mill in Mill Creek Park, Austin Log Cabin on Raccoon Road, Judge Newton's House now Parkview House Restaurant in Canfield, Newton presided over the first court session held in Mahoning County, First Mahoning County Courthouse of 1846 in Canfield, Camp Stambaugh Boy Scout Camp, Henry Kurz Monument in Springfield Township where the first printing press in that area was, Harper's Ferry Schoolhouse on Calla Road, Western Reserve Boundary Marker on State Line and Felger Roads, among others.

Requirements for the trail patch are at least 10 miles of cycling with an overnight stop at Camp Stambaugh.

MANCHESTER, ROBERT A. He was active in Scouting since his boyhood, becoming the third Scout to earn the Eagle Award in our council, became our Council President, served on the Regional and National Committee, received the Silver Beaver from our council and the Silver Antelope from the Region.

MARINO TRACT. Stambaugh acreage was increased by 28½ acres donated by Marguerite and Philanthropist Rocco E. Marino, June 1946. Total acreage for the Stambaugh Scout Reservation became 115.

The lower section of the Marino tract had not been used for camping because Indian Creek flooded bottom land approaches to it. In 1963, Marine Corps reserves drained the low land areas. Then they deepened and straightened the creek to prevent the flooding.

In 1963, a bridge made of three culverts was built over the creek and a slag road was laid to the tract of land. Syro Steel Company donated the culverts.

In 1964, three new campsites were built on the Marino tract. These are the Elm, Locust, and Chestnut campsites. Water lines were laid, toilet and washstand buildings were added.

MARTIN, HYER. Martin was a Field Scout Executive and a member of the camp staff in 1948 and 1949 in charge of the commissary. In 1950 he was camp director.

McKINLEY CABIN. The original building was built in the 1920s. It was an open sided shelter that was used as an outdoor kitchen pavilion with a fireplace at one end. Scouts camped in tents nearby and used the outdoor kitchen to prepare and eat meals. It was destroyed by fire in 1932.

Using the same foundation and fireplace, the McKinley cabin was built in 1938. A small kitchen was built on the back with a cast iron wood burner stove inside for cooking. The cabin was named after U.S. President William McKinley.

A handpump was located outside to the right of the cabin used to draw water until the 1970s.

The cabin was used for troop camping in the off season. During summer camp it was used in different years for nature, handicraft, staff quarters, and astronomy study.

Summer camp staffer Bill Kline painted star constellations on the ceiling of the McKinley cabin in the late 1960s using "glow paint". When the sky was not visible at night due to weather, Bill would charge the glow paint with a light bulb. When the light was turned off, the star constellations glowed. Scouts taking astronomy merit badge looked up at the ceiling while laying on bunk mattresses that were set on the floor. It worked very well.

Also in the late 1960s one night during the winter camping season, Troop 6 was camping in the McKinley cabin. The cabin had an old military surplus oil heater in it. But this night something backed up and the heater exploded. No one was hurt. But Scoutmaster Jack Sullivan recalls he and his Scouts had black soot scattered all over them and their gear.

The cabin was razed in 1987 due to decay.

MEINECKE, CONRAD. On November 11th, 1917, Conrad E. Meinecke became Council Executive to replace John Cross who didn't work out. This made Meinecke the first officially full-time paid Council Executive.

Born of sturdy pioneer parents in a northern Wisconsin Log cabin, his youth was spent ruggedly in the out-of-doors. Because he worked on a farm with his family, roamed the woods with the Indians, hiked across the prairies, climbed the rockies, fished in Canada, traveled in Europe, Asia Minor and north Africa, he learned how to make himself and his companions comfortable under all kinds of conditions. These experiences also taught him to understand and love mankind.

Conrad E. Meinecke was a cabin and wood craft builder. He did this as a hobby. He had scores of cabins that he built scattered over the United States and Canada.

Meinecke left our council September 1, 1923 for a similar position in Buffalo, New York.

After a few successful years in business once he left Scouting, Conrad decided to devote his life to the service of others through social work and maintained his contact with the great out doors. He received many requests to put all of his accumulated wisdom on the subject of cabin building into book form.

Meinecke wrote his first book titled "Your Cabin In The Woods". It was filled with cabin lore and his own simple philosophy of living. He printed the first edition on a small press in his home and bound it in cloth laced together with cord. Later in 1945 the book was published by Foster & Stewart Publishing Corporation at 210 Ellicott Street, Printed at the Airport Press in Buffalo, New York.

In the book "Your Cabin In The Woods", there are two pages of plans for the "Chiefs Cabin" that was built in Camp Stambaugh in 1919 on the north shore of Indian Creek. Meinecke designed and helped build this cabin from trees cut in camp.

Then in 1947, he wrote his second book titled, "Cabin Craft And Outdoor Living" also published by Foster & Stewart.

Conrad did not stop here. Wishing to maintain closer contact with his readers he formed the Darnock Cabin Craft Guild for the interchange of ideas between cabin builders. Membership was free and its members were scattered all over the world.

MEMBERSHIP.

YEAR	UNITS	YOUTH MEMBERS
*		
1914	*	300
*		
1927	51	1,144
*		
1947	*	2,691
1948	144	2,809
1949	148	3,238

1950	158	4,147
1951	150	4,027
1952	131	3,657
1953	135	3,967
1954	150	4,390
1955	164	4,935
1956	182	5,592
1957	172	5,474
1958	167	5,697
1959	183	5,710
1960	204	5,982
1961	206	5,915
1962	195	6,028
1963	200	6,217
1964	214	6,417
1965	188	6,417
1966	180	5,588
1967	181	5,926
1968	191	6,150
1969	203	6,369
*		
1976	125	3,416
1977	108	3,159
1978	107	2,698
1979	104	2,640
1980	105	2,515
1981	107	2,318
1982	94	2,596
1983	93	2,458
1984	94	2,417
1985	93	2,381
1986	82	2,072
1987	88	2,110
1988	93	2,565
1989	94	2,581
1990	94	2,423
1991	79	2,452
1992	82	2,455
1993 to March 1st.	80	2,283

MIKKELSON, DON AND GLADYS. Don and Gladys Mikkelson with their five children moved into Camp Stambaugh's Ranger's Home August, 1955. Don served as Camp Ranger for 24 years and Gladys was summer camp cook for many of those years.

Don joined Scouting at age 12 in 1929 and had 50 years in Scouting by the time he retired August, 1979.

During an interview with Don, he recalled, "One day we were playing ball on the street when a man named Mr. Fear came up, looked at us and said, 'Are any of you fellows about twelve years old'? Some of us raised our hands and said 'yes, we're twelve years old'. Mr. Fear said, 'Well, I'm starting a Boy Scout troop up at the end of the street, and I need you fellows'. 'A Boy Scout troop' I said, 'Why that's only for sissies'. He looked at us, laughed and said, "Do sissies go overnight camping? Do sissies cook out? Do sissies go on hikes?' We told him we would talk it over, and that night we went to the meeting at the end of the street. Sure enough he was right. We enjoyed it.

As time went on our troop camped in Camp Stambaugh. I used to tease Camp Ranger Harry Walker by telling him, 'Some day when I grow up, I'm going to have your job in camp'. Harry replied, 'Well son, you never can tell!" Later on, Don became a Scoutmaster and before taking the position as camp ranger, he worked for the U.S. Forest Service in Idaho.

Don said, "Today's youth seem more motivated than the Scouts of 20 years ago. The youngsters are ambitious."

Gladys said, "It (Camp Stambaugh) was a wonderful place to live and raise a family. We have watched boys grow into men."

Gladys always told the scouts, "If you get lost in camp, remember that every path leads to the kitchen".

I remember serving as Don's Indian Guide for his Vigil honor in the Order of the Arrow.

Don and Gladys have always been very special and warm friends of mine.

MILL CREEK PARK SCOUT TRAIL. In May of 1962, the Boy Scout trail was added to Mill Creek Park. It was designed to help Scouts pass some 2nd Class requirements at that time. Scouts had to hike at least five miles, cook a meal, and then clean up. Those in charge of creating the trail were: Council Executive Henry Katschke, Assistant Council Executive Stu Rila, and Park Superintendent Al Davies.

MOYER HEALTH LODGE. The Moyer Health Lodge was built in the summer of 1967 and dedicated that August. The lodge was named in honor of Sidney Moyer and built on the same site as the Walnut cabin.

At that time, Sidney Moyer was the only Scout Leader in the council with 50 years continuous service. He helped organize Troop 19 at Rodef Sholom Temple in 1912. He was District Commissioner and on the Executive Board from 1929 - 1954.

The Truscon Manufacturing division of Republic Steel Corporation donated the pre-fabricated steel structure. Sidney Moyer donated $5,000 necessary for the construction of the lodge.

(1) Conrad Meinecke. First Council Executive (1917-1923). **(2)** Sidney Moyer, 1967. **(3-5)** Conrad Meinecke's first book, "Your Cabin In The Woods", published in 1945. In the book there are two pages (photo #4) of plans for the "Chief's Cabin" (photo #5) that Meinecke designed and help build in Camp Stambaugh in 1919. (photo 5, Frondorf album, circa 1940s). **(6)** Meinecke's second book published in 1947 titled: "Cabin Craft And Outdoor Living". **(7)** Moyer Health Lodge, 1967. **(8)** McKinley cabin, 1950. **(9)** Culvert bridge connecting the Marino Tract to the Stambaugh Reservation, 1963. (photos 2,7,9 by Lee Banks). **(10)** Robert A. Manchester, Council President, 1948-1953.

3

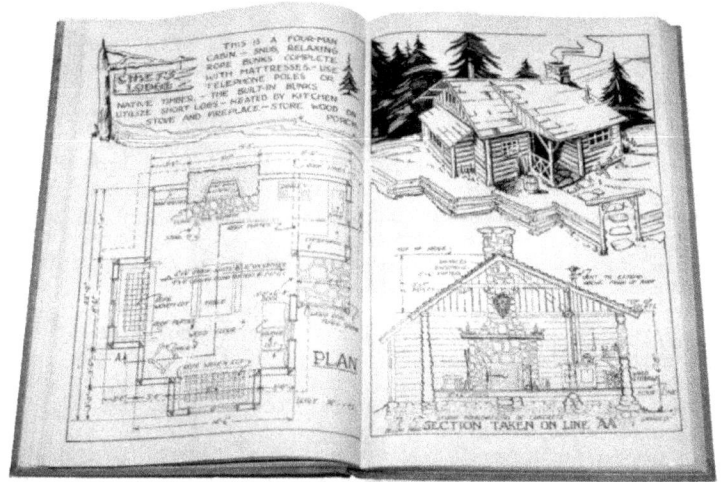

4

5

6

7

8

9

10

ORDER OF THE ARROW. The Order of the Arrow (O.A.) was founded in 1915 by Dr. E. Urner Goodman at the Philadelphia Scout Camp, Treasure Island. It is a youth organization consisting of honor campers. Members are elected by their troop.

The O.A. Lodge in Mahoning Valley Council was first chartered in 1948. The Lodge was known as #396. There wasn't a name for the Lodge in 1948, 1949, and 1950.

In 1951 and 1952, Council Executive Henry Katschke refused to re-charter the Lodge because of an incident that took place regarding initiation.

In 1953, our O.A. Lodge was named "Mahoning Lodge".

On Monday October 14, 1957, the Order of the Arrow Executive Committee held a meeting in the Katschke Lodge in Camp Stambaugh to reorganize the Lodge. They talked about changing the O.A. Lodge name from "Mahoning Lodge, #396" to "Neatoka Lodge, #396".

The meeting was conducted by Vice-Chief Jim Wilhide. Among those attending were A.D. Hamilton, John Wolboldt Jack Sullivan, Randall Hively, Lodge Advisor Harry Hunter, Ken Strawn, John Dodge, George Woodman, Fred Altdoefer, Dan Wolboldt. David Reichard made the following motion: "The name of this lodge shall be Neatoka, meaning Council Rock in the language of the Delaware Indian, and that the lodge totem be a council rock with red lightning striking it". A simple flap patch was designed with white background, yellow border, gray rock with red lightning striking it, red "WWW", and black "Neatoka Lodge 396".

In 1958 the Lodge was re-chartered as "Neatoka Lodge #396" and the lodge newsletter was titled Arrowflight.

In 1959, the O.A. constructed a Personal Fitness Course as a service project in Camp Stambaugh. It was located between the Aspen Campsite and Leffingwell Road. Maintenance of the course was done by the O.A. through the 1960s and 1970s.

Youth Ordeal Masters were first used on September 14, 1959. Prior, adults were used.

"Allogagan" means, He who serves. In 1967 a bead recognition program was started by the lodge for Arrowmen who served. The bead representations follow. WHITE for Ordeal membership. RED for Brotherhood membership. BRASS for Vigil membership. BLUE for Annual Dinner attendance. ORANGE for Service Project completion. BLACK for Spring Fellowship attendance. YELLOW for Fall Fellowship attendance. GREEN for Ceremonial Team participation, and TURQUOISE for Dance Team participation.

In 1967, a large wooden O.A. flap patch was made and erected on top of the telescope cabin which was used by the O.A. Arrowmen working on the project were Pat Ravotti, Jim Swaney, Mike Dyer, Mike Liptay, Mike Sankey, Jim Deckant, and Bill Kline.

In the 1968 close-out report of Council Executive Henry Katshchke at the time of his retirement, he wrote: "The staff advisor is Bart Ingram. Bart is gradually getting the chapter (Neatoka Lodge, #396) in hand and operating properly. It takes constant watching because many adults in the council are constantly taking over whenever and whereever possible. It is really not the organization for boys as it has been intended to be. At the present time (1968) the boys are only the "front". There are the adults who are determined that even though they are not at the meeting, the boys will consult with them".

In 1969 at a Fall Fellowship, a totem pole was carved by the O.A. and placed on the island in Indian Lake.

The first Neatoka Lodge, #396 "Trad-O-Ree and Scout Memorabilia" auction began in 1976 under the direction of Walter Fowles. The purpose of this auction which became an annual event was for fellowship and to raise money for camperships in order to provide partial scholarships to needy Scouts who wish to attend summer camp. The money went to the A.D. Hamilton Memorial Campership Fund.

In 1984, the Section 5-B Conclave was held at Stambaugh May 4-6.

The O.A. always had a cabin in camp that could be heated when used and where ceremonial and dance costumes could be stored. The larger cabins allowed room for meetings and even a few bunks for overnighters. The O.A. used the following cabins: (1) 1948-1987, telescope cabin. (2) 1950s-1970s, Katschke Lodge. (3) 1977-1986, Schwebel Lodge. (4) 1986-1989, Hunter Lodge.

Neatoka Lodge is one of the few lodges in the country that has a real existing totem. It is a large rock known as "Council Rock" in Lincoln Park. The park is located on the east side of town near Landsdowne Boulevard and Oak Street off of Shehy Street. It is a place in the park where the Seneca, Shawnee, Mingoe, and Delaware Indians gathered to celebrate their victory over General Washington, who had come from Williamsburg, West Virginia to drive the French and Indians from Fort Duquesne at the junction of the Allegheny and Monogahela Rivers.

During the celebration, legend has it that, lightning struck the rock, split it in two, and killed four Chiefs and more than three hundred braves. The Council Rock is our Lodge totem and is also the central part of our Lodge patch and neckerchief.

In a book titled, "History of Youngstown & The Mahoning Valley, Ohio" by Joseph G. Butler, Jr., Volume I, 1921, page 93, 94, there is the legend of Council Rock.

It is rewritten from an original story that was first printed in the late 1800s by William G. Conner. He was a pioneer resident of Dry Run Valley in which Lincoln Park is located.

Mr. Conner relates while on a hunting trip, he met an old trapper named Mr. Dunlap who knew the Dry Run Valley very well. Dunlap had been on a surveying party in the summer of 1796 to help survey Township Two, Range Two of the Connecticut Reserve for John Young (founder of Youngstown).

During the survey, Mr. Dunlap and his party found two French-Canadian Trappers in the Valley of the Dry Run. They told Dunlap that what is now the Eastern Part of Youngstown was a favorite meeting place for the Indians. That three times a year the Indians held celebrations and feasts and gathered near a large rock known as Nea-To-Ka, or Council Rock. The Trappers told Dunlap that as much as 3,500 Indians belonging to the Seneca, Shawnee, Mingo & Delaware tribes would assemble at Council Rock but because of what occurred in the summer of 1755 caused them to leave the area.

It was during a celebration that a violent wind suddenly descended on the meeting. It knocked everything down in a 200 yard path. It knocked over trees and killed squaws and children. Suddenly a flash of lightning struck in the middle of the feasting braves, splitting the great rock and killing four of the chiefs.

Fearing they may have displeased the Great Spirit, they buried their dead and hurried away. This was the last recorded council at the rock.

LEGEND

Long years ago in the dim ages of the past, the Lenni Lenape Tribe of the Delaware Indians inhabited the Delaware River Valley. They hunted and fished; pursued the deer, the bear, the wildcat, and the panther. Their villages were numerous and powerful; their hunting parties strong. They tilled the fields as well as the chase. They were peaceful people; the smoke arose from their wigwams as they returned from the hunt.

Many moons they lived in this blissful state of happy contentment. Springtime blossomed into summer, matured into autumn, and faded away into winter, in what seemed a never ending succession of season. But a cloud arose on the scene. Neighboring tribes and distant enemies began to raid their hunting grounds. Then Chingachgook, the mighty chief, made inquiry, "Who will go and warn the villages of the Delawares of the danger which threatens?" But none wished to go. One, Uncas, his son, said, "My father, here am I; send me. All these villages are of our blood--Lenni Lenape. What is danger to one is the affair of all. The need is urgent. They are six to our one, and if we are to survive as a nation, we must all stand by each other. Meanwhile let us both urge upon our kindred the necessity of unselfish devotion to each other and the cause in which we are enlisted, and as they get this higher vision, send them forth on their errand of cheerful service."

Then Chingachgook, the chief, and his son Uncas, set to work. In every village were found some who were willing to give themselves cheerfully in the service of others. Their enemies were compelled to retire to their own borders, and when peace was declared between them, they who first went out cheerfully to save their kindred were raised to places of high eminence in the tribe by the chief. For he said, "The servant of all is the greatest of all." And these men became so convinced of the truth of this saying that they besought the chief to perpetuate it in some manner.

So Chingachgook bound them together in a Brotherhood into which only they can be admitted who can forget their own interests and advancement while looking out for those of their brothers. And these must be so considered and recommended for membership by their associates.

So greatly did this Order aid and strengthen the Lenni Lenape that other tribes seeing this besought their help in forming similar lodges in their own tribes. So in the same spirit of service many such lodges were formed, which were bound together into a great brotherhood.

And so we, the followers of the early Indian on this soil, perpetuate to the present day the Brotherhood of Cheerful Service, which being translated into the Delaware Indians, becomes Wimachtendienk (wee-mock-ten-dink), Wingolauchsik (Wing-o-loss-ik), Witahemui (wit-a-hem-a-way).

LODGE CHIEFS

1956-1957	Alan Axelson
1958	Jim Wilhide
1959	Edward Kusky
1960	Grier Richardson
1961	Mike Dyer
1962	Mike Ullman
1963	Mike Blott
1964	Larry Jeffies
1965	Ed Folkwein
1966	Russ Miklos
1967	Mike Sankey
1968	Bill Kline
1969	Mike Sankey
1970	Ken Goist
1971	Bill Knight
1972	Jim Brammer
1973	Dennis Oblinger
1974	Jim Brammer
1975	John Foss
1976	Dale Beckman
1977	Robert Kneen
1978	William Merz

1979	Jeff Holiday
1980	Jim Hegedusich
1981	Bob Gingery
1982-1983	Steve Ramos
1984	Glen Norling
1985	Greg Puhalla
1986	Terry Mock
1987	Kevin Bokesch
	(Bokesch elected Section Vice-Chief)
1988	Kevin Bokesch
	(Bokesch elected Section Chief)
1989	John Paul Shippert
	(Bokesch elected Region Chief)
1990	John Starkey
1991	Tony Garcia
1992	Mike Metcalf

LODGE ADVISORS

1948-1950	unknown
1951-1952	Lodge was not chartered
1953-1954	unknown
1956-1959	Harry Hunter
	(retired Council Executive)
1960-1961	John Wolboldt
1962-1965	unknown
1966-1972	Joe Roble
1972-1973	Chet Taylor
1974	Joe Johnson Sr.
1975-1977	Chuck Kneen
1978-1979	Tony Valley Jr.
1980-1982	Dallas Heston
1983	Jeff Dyer
1984-1985	Glen Michaels
1986-1991	Dale Beckman
1992-1993	Joe Taucher

VIGIL MEMBERS
(Year, Member, Indian Name, Meaning)

1959
Council Executive Harry Hunter .... *
(from another council)

1960
John Wolboldt .... Go To Kow Pah A,
He Who Stands Alone
Jim Wilhide .... Afanata,
The Man At The Helm

1961
A.D. Hamilton .... Ro'Heh Hon,
Energetic Man
Dan Wolboldt .... Mesa Min Ka Ki,
Singing Long Time

1962
Council Executive Henry Katschke .... Sakima,
Chief
Warren Host .... Ches II Hong Ha,
Has Good Sense
Mike Dyer .... Ga Li'La Hi,
Amiable One
Merrill Price .... Quog'Quish,
The Runner

1964
Mike Blott .... Klamach Pin,
Quiet One
Ed Dyer .... Ka'Ge Zhin Ga,
Little Brother
Al Schrecengost .... Ma'To Po Tan'Ka,
Bear With Big Voice

1967
Pat Ravotti .... Wulelendam,
Cheerful One
Joe Roble .... Wulaeschi'Molsin,
The Friendly One
Tim Bowser .... Benda'Goga,

		The Bender of the Bow
Bob Kasmer	....	Wu Lis'So, Handsome One
Bill Wolboldt	....	Ha'Ie No Nis, Music Maker
Jerimy Burdge	....	Okyoli Imponna, Swimmer

1968
Mike Sankey .... Mikemossit, The Worker

1969-1971
None

1972
Bill Nell .... Tsungani, Excels All Others
Jim Brammer .... Mon E'Gahi, Arrow Chief
Tony Valley Jr .... Tye Daka Rih'Hon, The Flying Messenger
Ed Enterline .... Masch'Kaow Peme Bea, He who Strongly Paddles The Canoe

1974
Rick Jugenheimer .... Apela, Helper
Dennis Oblinger .... Y Ush'Bo Nu Li, The Dancer
John Foss .... Tah Kah'Enhyunk, Looks Both Ways
John Kneen .... Naga'Tamen, Reliable One

1975
Charles Rischar .... Tayanita, Young Beaver
Harry Pancher .... Ho'Sa Ho Ho, Large Mouth
Dale Beckman .... Achpequot, Wounded One

1976
Jeff Dyer .... Man Cha Tan Ka Ne Do'Gonah, Guide Among The Pines
Bob Kneen .... Nan Se Us Kuk, The Whirling Thunder
John Holderman .... Koo Koo Ku'Hoo, Owl
Gary Chrislip .... Akikta, Works With Determination

1977
Tom Chickonoski .... Tgauchsin, Good Natured One
William Merz .... Lachauweleman, He Who Is Concerned
Robert Gingery .... Klamhattenamin, One Of Calm Mind
Chuck Kneen .... Wetochwink, One Who Is Father To Many
Murle McLaughlin .... Manachewagan, Cutter Of Wood
Don Mikkelson .... Wilawi, Valuable One

1978
William Hegedusich .... Aponaklo, An Inquirer
Jeff Holiday .... Etilkissin, Laughing One
Sandor Tollas .... Pohonasin, Drum Beater
Walter Fowles .... Memhallmund, The Trader
Robert Roberts .... A Khi Ko'Ka, One Who Is Skillful

1979
Brian Bishop .... Ne'Pauz Pash'Pish Au, Rising Sun
Warren Weller .... Tschitanitehen, Perservering One
Perry Chickonoski .... Anatshiton, One Who Cares
Lou Chicchillo .... Anumpuli, Counselor

1980
Jim Hegedusich .... Welauchist, Orderly One
Mike Balaban .... Hoh Squa Sa Ga-Dah, The Woodsman

1981
Dave Hegedusich .... Witscheman, Helpful One

1982
Mark Puhalla .... Machelesin, High Minded One
Jon Ripple .... Kuwe, Pine Tree
Steve Ramos .... Yukpa, Merry One

1983
Craig Puhalla .... Aiokpachi Achukman, Diligent One
Dallas Heston .... Kwas, Woodpecker
Glen Norling .... Ksinelendam, Carefree

1984
None

1985
Craig Susany .... Uga Shon'ton, Traveler
Jeff Solic .... Lungwamen, Dreamer
Glen Michaels .... Clam Hatten Moagan, Steady One.

1986
None

1987
Michael Walsh .... Wewingtonheet, Talker
Patrick Walsh .... Chans, Elder Brother
Steve Domonkos .... Sachgachton, Cook

1988
Kevin Bokesch .... La Wahee Coots La Shaw No, The Brave Chief
Kevin Urichich .... Hatak Kamassa, Strong Man
Mark Hradil .... A Yun Li, First In The Dance

1989
William D. Hunt Sr .... *

William F. Hunt Jr .... *

Michael Lamparty .... *

1990-1992
None

OSCAR PROGRAM. The Oscar Program started under Council Executive Conrad Meinecke circa 1916 and continued through the terms of Council Executives Harry Hunter, K.L. Brown, and Henry Katschke. It was a program through which the Youngstown Rotary Club presented a trophy to the Scoutmaster of the outstanding troop.

In 1951, the council executive board accepted the recommendation of the commissioners that a program be devised whereby all packs, troops and posts could qualify. The Youngstown Rotary Club continued to support the program. The Knights of Columbus agreed

to present the statuettes to Packs. Later the B'nai B'rith Lodge also supported this program. This program was well received by the council leaders.

OUTRIDERS. The Outriders was an activities committee in Pioneer District of older Scouts where six boys were in charge. The program was designed to give older Scouts responsibility, teach leadership, teach teamwork, and build character. Their primary duties were to serve as Commissioners in the district and help troops in whatever way they could and to plan and be responsible for district events such as training courses, Camporees, Klondike Derbys, and other district events without adult participation.

The Outriders was created in the spring of 1975 by District Executive Fred Baird, District Activities Chairman Tony Valley Jr. and Committee Member Joe Angelo Sr. Joe and I (Tony) were the only adults involved serving as advisors to the Outriders.

The Outriders were first announced May 10, 1975 at the Pioneer District Camporee in Big Oak. The Outriders planned, prepared logistics and staffed the event.

Scouts from various troops would sign up with the Outriders as a specialist for a certain skill or skills and can be called upon any time to assist.

(1) Dr. E. Urner Goodman, 1979. Founder of the Order of the Arrow. (photo by author). (2) Kevin Bokesch, 1989. Only Arrowman in our lodge to be elected Region Chief. (photo by Jack Acri). (3) First known lodge flap patch, designed in 1957. (4) "Council Rock", the lodge totem, in Lincoln Park, 1987. Pictured are: Lodge Chief Kevin Bokesch (top), (from left) Vice Chief Kevin Urichich, Secretary Jerry Land, Executive Vice Chief Mike Walsh, and Treasurer Bill Morris. Note the separation in the rock at left behind Kevin Urichich. (photo by author). (5) The telescope cabin used by the O.A. from 1948-1987. (photo by author, 1985). (6) O.A. Dance Team Advisor Jerry Stanovcak, 1976.

P **PAGEANT.** The Pageant was developed as a campfire entertainment around 1931. Campers dressed and played different roles depicting the advancement of camping. It was performed every camp period.

PARKER, THEODORE J. Jr. Ted, as he was known, was Council Executive of Mahoning Valley Council from November 1974 until his death June 2, 1985.

A native of Birmingham, Alabama, he began his professional Scouting career December 1950 as field executive in Columbus Georgia. In 1952 he joined the staff in Atlanta Georgia in the same position. In 1958 he transferred to Miami Florida and 1965 to Cincinnati Ohio in charge of special projects. In 1970 Ted joined the National staff in the Professional Training Division. November of 1974, he was selected as Council Executive for our council.

Ted was known for his innovative approach and work with education, and minority migrants. He was well known as an outdoorsman and was described by the Philadelphia Inquirer as a leather-skinned, gravel-voiced cross between Davey Crockett and a Grizzly Bear.

While serving Scouting in Alabama, he created the "Scoutmobile" program for the Gila River Indian Community. He brought Scouting to their remote area. As a tribute to Ted, one of his Scouts made a 20"x30" framed drawing of Ted and his Scoutmobile.

Here in Mahoning Valley Council, he was in part responsible for the purchase of the Swanston Estate. His dream was to develop this property for high adventure Scouting and training, but he died before the purchase was finalized.

He was married to Catherine and had three children.

PHILMONT SCOUT RANCH. Philmont is a national camping area that is owned and operated by the Boy Scouts of America. It comprises 137,493 acres or about 215 square miles of rugged mountain wilderness in the Sangre de Cristo range of the Rocky Mountains in northern New Mexico.

In the 1920s, Oklahoma oilman Waite Phillips purchased a part of the Mexican land grant that was made to Charles Beaubien and Don Guadalupe Miranda. Waite Phillips built his ranch on this land. In 1941 he presented part of it to the National Council of the Boy Scouts of America for high adventure training. It received the name Philmont from the words PHILlip's MOuNTains.

Over 15,000 older Scouts and leaders each year come to Philmont. Some to backpack the high mountains which dominate rough terrain with elevations ranging from 6,500 to 12,441 feet. Some come to Philmont for training at the training center.

PIONEER DISTRICT CAMPOREE AT BIG OAK. On the weekend of May 9-11, 1975, 125 Pioneer District Scouts and 45 leaders attended the "Orienteering" Spring Camporee that was planned and executed by the district Outriders with advisors Tony Valley and Joe Angelo Sr. All events revolved around reading a topographic map and compass.

'Friday night at the Movies' opened the Camporee with a film strip on compass, map reading and orienteering followed by singing and other goodies while Scouts sat on a hillside overlooking the valley.

On Saturday, five stations were demonstrative and competitive. Station one, manned by Rick Zenn and Mike Silleck, was Dutch Oven cooking. Station two, manned by Dennis Dorinski and Rodney Lyndon, was various ways of making fires and a string burning competition. Station three was the fun station of communications where walkie-talkies were used to radio back to camporee headquarters using all those fancy radio terms and proper use of a radio. They liked this station, "Roger Dodger" and all that. Station four, manned by Nick Valley and Mike O'Reilly, was the most interesting. It was making and using snares and traps in a survival situation using nothing more than what nature provided. Station five, manned by Jerry Angelo Jr. and Ron Wick, was using rope as a windless and a winch without using a block and tackle.

After Scouts were at their third station around lunch time, the staff demonstrated utensiless cooking with an orange, potato, ½ pound of bear meat, snake meat or anything else you want to call it, two buns and some seasoning. The orange was cut in half and the inside eaten out. The bear meat was rolled in the hand and with onion and other seasoning and placed, ¼ pound each, in each orange half and placed on the hot coals to cook. The meat absorbs an orange flavor. The potato was simply buried under the coals with no wrapping. If it is buried completely removed from the air, it won't burn.

Later in the afternoon, a campwide compass game was played where no two troops followed the same course. District Executive Fred Baird watched from top of a distant hill. "There were 125 Scouts scrambling across each others path, zigging here and zagging there. It sure looked like fun!"

After supper, the staff went to each Troop to judge skits and points were awarded. The top 3 skits at the camporee were played at the Saturday evening campfire.

The campfire was a real treat. Hundreds of paper bags with a lit candle in each lined the path to the campfire site on the side of a natural amphitheater. Millions of stars in the sky could be seen and the moon silhouetted the horizon on the far hillside.

The fire was started and the Pioneer District Outrider boy leader program was introduced for the first time. The best 3 skits were played and awards for the days events were given.

Towards the end of the campfire, Mike Silleck read the history of Scouting between two torches, and then came the surprise. 'Baden Powell' came forth out of the darkness with campaign hat and cape, to read his farewell message he wrote before dying. Silence filled the campfire and the true meaning and feeling of fellowship that Scouting created that weekend was felt by all.

Long time friend and Scouter, Mike Balaban, played the part of Baden Powell and even had the seasoned adult leaders second guessing themselves.

When Baden Powell turned and left after his farewell message, the entire Camporee stood and sang the National Anthem as the American flag, while spotlighted, flew across the valley upon a hill. Actually, there was no wind that night, so we had a couple of Scouts pull a rope back and forth that was tied to the corner of the flag.

Theodore Parker, Council Executive, 1974-1985.

55

RAUSCHENBACH FLAGPOLE, EMIL. On June 14, 1968, Troop 38 dedicated a fifty foot metal flag pole at the top of the hill in Camp Stambaugh near the parking lot. It honors Emil Rauschenbach for over 40 years of service as Scoutmaster to that troop at Pleasant Grove United Presbyterian Church. Emil at that time was in his 48th year of Scouting.

REFORESTING STAMBAUGH SCOUT RESERVATION. In 1919 the Stambaugh Reservation was open fields. The creek at the bottom of the farm could be seen from the old red barn where the K.L. Brown Pavilion now stands. Only fruit orchards and meadows existed.

The first conservation project to plant trees on the reservation began. Mr. Meyer from Ritter and Meyer along with his wife, Helen Strouss Meyer, financed the first reforesting of the Stambaugh Scout Reservation.

RELIGIOUS COMMITTEES ON SCOUTING. The purpose of these committees is to supplement the spiritual program of the Boy Scouts of America.

The first Protestant Committee On Scouting in Mahoning Valley Council was appointed in the early 1950s by the Council of Churches Executive Director Dr. Paul Gauss after a visit from Council President Robert Manchester and Council Executive Henry E. Katschke. The Protestant Committee On Scouting assigned the first Camp Stambaugh Summer Camp Chaplain the following season.

The Catholic Committee On Scouting in the Mahoning Valley Council was also appointed in the early 1950s.

There had been previous attempts to bring a closer working relationship between Scouting in the council and the Catholic Church, but it wasn't until 1949 when Bishop Walsh was assigned to the Youngstown Diocese that a Catholic Committee On Scouting was formed. Bishop Walsh had a great interest in the Boy Scout Program and a desire to see the program in more of the parishes.

The Catholic Committee On Scouting sponsored the Annual Sisters Day At Stambaugh and the Annual Awards Night at St. Columba.

The objective of the Catholic Committee On Scouting is to help make the Scouting program available in Catholic sponsored units. The committee has also been responsible for promoting programs for other religions that have no such committee.

St. GEORGE AWARD

The St. George Award is a national recognition approved by the National Catholic Committee on Scouting. It may be presented to any adult who is working in the Scout program who has made a significant contribution to Scouting in the field of Catholic relationships. It can be awarded to women, priests, religious or non-Catholics.

The purpose of this program is to recognize the recipient's outstanding contribution to the spiritual development of Catholic youth in the program of the Boy Scouts of America.

The following are the recipients of the St. George Award and the year it was awarded:

1956	Frank J. Bertch
1958	William Storey
1959	Emil Palguta
1960	Ralph Dillon
	Philip H. Stratford
1961	John Herrlich
1962	Andrew Wren
1963-1966	none
1967	Ted Gavozzi

1968	none
1969	Most Reverend James W. Malone (Bishop of Youngstown)
	Franklin Ernst
	Joseph Herrlich
1970	John Kundracik
	Judge John Leskovyansky
1971	Anthony Vivo
1972	Louis Birckbichler
1973	Charles Gray
1974	Joseph Novotny
1975	Clarence E. Potts Jr.
1976	Rudy Hudak
1977	Michael Balaban
	Martin D. Lipkovich
1978	Louis Cicchillo
	Henry Sforza
1979	Ray Cunning
1980	Alex Seka
1981	Joseph Angelo
	Fred David
1982	Don Davis
1983	Dr. John LeBrun
1984	John Holderman
	Stephen Seifert
1985	Robert Puhalla
1986	Walter Wills
	Fr. Jerome J. Conroy
1987	James Driscoll
	Most Reverend Benedict Franzetta (Auxiliary Bishop of Youngstown)
1988	Ralph McDonough
1989	*
1990	Terry Daprile
	Brother Leon Mancinelli
1991	none
1992	Marty Gilboy
1993	John Stroney

BRONZE PELICAN AWARD

The "Bronze Pelican Award" is awarded to leaders involved in Scouting for their outstanding contribution to the spiritual development of Catholic youth in the program of Scouting.

Recipients of the award must be exemplary individuals who are active and certified by their local Scout council as registered Scouters currently serving in active positions, and these recipients must have full approval of their respective pastors before the award is given.

The following are the recipients of the Bronze Pelican Award and the year it was awarded:

1980	Fred David
1979	Don Davis
	John Holderman
1982	Robert Cicchillo
1983	Fr. Jerome J. Conroy
	Steve Seifert
1984	Robert Puhalla
	Joseph Kolat
1985	Tony Valley Jr.
1986	Brother Leon Mancinelli
	James Driscoll Sr.
1987	Ralph J. McDonough
	Marty Gilboy
1988	Terry Daprile
	John Stroney
1989	George Grimm
1990	Harold Gallagher
	Richard Hart
1991	Art Bosker
1992	Mike Kupec
	Jim Driscoll Jr.

RICHARDS, STEVE. Was an Outrider and a Scout from Troop 38. He died accidentally November 20, 1975, after his 14th birthday.

RIFLE RANGE. Its not known when the rifle range was originally built. The side of a sandy bank was used as the target backstop. Sand from this bank was also used for the mortar in the construction of some of the cabins in camp.

Until 1955, a canvas shelter was pitched over the wooden shooting platform. In 1955 the rifle range was refurbished because it was in bad condition. A wooden roof was added to the shooting platform and a thick metal backdrop was installed behind the target area.

ROOSEVELT CABIN. The Roosevelt cabin was named after U.S. President, Teddy Roosevelt. The cabin was built in 1928 on the south side of the lake along the trail west of the Wick Lodge. The cabin was at the crest of a hill along the trail near a large double tree.

The Roosevelt cabin was used as a nature lodge during summer camp and a camping cabin during the off season.

It had running water from a spring that ran into the cabin through a pipe from the side of the hill behind the cabin.

On March 2, 1953 the cabin burned to the ground. Rock remnants from the foundation can still be seen at the site.

ROSTER OF TROOPS IN 1933. The roster of Mahoning Valley Council in 1933 follows:

TROOP #	YEAR	PLACE OF ORIGINATION
1	1918	Christ Mission and Kiwanis Club
2	1926	West Side Baptist Mission
3	1930	St. Mark's Lutheran
4	1918	Richard Brown Memorial Church
5	1917	Epworth Church
6	1919	South U.P. Church
8	1920	Bethlehem Church
9	1912	First Presbyterian Church
10	1924	St. Paul's Church
11	1918	Brownlee Woods Church
12	1918	Truscon Steel Company
13	1929	Foster Memorial Church
14	1918	Hillman Street Church
15	1926	Trinity Methodist Church
16	1924	Struthers U.P. Church
17	1919	McGuffey Memorial Church
18	1920	West Side Citizens
19	1912	Rodef Sholem Temple
20	1927	St. Luke's Church
21	1927	Calvary Church
22	1932	St. Andrew's Church
24	1919	Oak Hill Avenue A.M.E. Church
25	1926	Canfield Religious Educational Council
26	1927	Methodist Protestant Church
28	1919	St. Edward's Church
30	1930	Swedish Mission Church
31	1920	Tabernacle Church
32	1926	Magyar Evangelical Reformed Church
33	1930	North Side Baptist Chapel
34	1924	Central Christian Church
35	1927	Pearl Street Mission
36	1927	St. John's Church
37	1930	Christ's Mission Settlement
38	1922	Pleasant Grove Church
39	1922	Glenwood Home and Kiwanis Club
40	1930	Caldwell Settlement
43	1927	Struther's American Legion

TROOP #	YEAR	PLACE OF ORIGINATION
44	1923	Poland Presbyterian Church
45	1924	Mahoning Avenue Church
46	1931	Boardman Methodist Church
48	1923	Temple Emmanuel
50	1931	St. Brendan's Church
51	1931	American Leagion
53	1927	St. Dominic"s Church
54	1927	Third Reformed Church
55	1928	First Christian Church
56	1928	Grace Lutheran Church
57	1928	Sacred Heart Church
58	1928	Grace Methodist Church
59	1928	St. Patrick's Church
60	1928	Westminster Church
61	1932	Himrod Avenue Church
62	1931	St. Elizabeth's Church
65	1932	Baptist Temple
66	1928	Faith Church
70	1928	St. Joseph's Church
73	1928	Sebring Church of Christ
74	1929	Sebring Methodist Church
75	1929	Sebring U.P. Church
80	1931	Deerfield Methodist Church
83	1930	West Austintown Church
84	1929	Austintown Community Church
85	1930	North Jackson Federated Church
86	1928	Struther's Methodist Church
87	1928	Struther's Lutheran Church
90	1930	Struther's Congregational Church
91	1932	Struther's Baptist Church
97	1928	Lowellville Presbyterian Church
98	1928	Lowellville American Legion
99	1918	Hubbard Kiwanis Club
100	1928	Hubbard High School
102	1928	Hubbard Citizens

ROUNDTABLE MEETING. The first council roundtable meeting was planned and arranged by the Scout Leaders Club in 1930 and held in the Scouter Cabin.

ROVERS. Baden Powell had started a program for Senior Scouts called the "Rovering" program. In 1930 this program was being used by our council. It became known as "Rovers".

The Rover program was for Life Scouts who were advanced campers and who had done everything else offered at Camp Stambaugh.

The Rovers traveled to other Scout camps including Akron, Canton, Wheeling, and other areas. They traveled in a stake-body truck with a top made out of tree saplings bent in a covered wagon fashion and covered with canvas. A second and much older truck followed with equipment and supplies. The Rovers' activities involved requirements from the following merit badges: cooking, camping, leatherwork, leathercraft, knifecraft, and axemanship. Special training was provided in: self-control, self-reliance, initiative, and citizenship. Fun activities included: camp fires, games, songs, stories, ball games, and swimming.

Rover director was Hernan Brandmiller III. He also served as Associate Council Executive.

Assistant to the Rover director was assistant Scoutmaster David Linebaugh of Troop 43 and of Struthers High School.

(1) Troop 38 Scoutmaster, Emil Rauschenbach at age 73 in 1973. (2) Stu Rila, 1963, Assistant Council Executive. (3) Thomas Richardson, 1966. (photo by Lee Banks). (4) Roosevelt cabin, 1940s. (5) Roosevelt cabin shortly after it burned down in the evening of March 2, 1953. The trail parallel to the lake is to the right. (6) Rifle Range shooting platform with canvas shelter, 1950. (photo by Ernest Grass). (7) Field Sports Director Tom Reed at the Rifle Range teaches Scouts from Troop 105 of North Jackson, 1967. Ronald Pal (left), and Fred Eichhorn. (Vindicator). (8) Rovers in 1930 returning to Camp Stambaugh from a trip during 2nd period of camp.

SCHWEBEL MEMORIAL LODGE. When Dave Schwebel first heard of the council's 1962 long range program for Camp Stambaugh, he said, "I think this is something my brothers and sisters would be interested in, a lodge where boys and men could get together in pleasant surroundings, learn about Scouting, nature, and the stars."

The Schwebel Memorial Lodge was built and later dedicated on September 24th, 1965 by Dave Schwebel and his brother and sisters. It was the same design as the Wallis Lodge.

It served as the camp office during summer camp season in the late 1960s.

In 1977, the interior of the lodge was refurbished by the Order of the Arrow. They used it for their lodge until 1986 when they moved into the Hunter cabin.

SCOUT CAPADES. In 1958, some 3,000 local Cub, Boy and Explorer Scouts representing 96 units, staged a two hour, 10 act production called "Scout Capades". It took place on Thursday, Friday and Saturday, November 20-22 in the Struthers Field House at 7:30pm. The theme was "Boys Today - Men Tomorrow".

Representatives from newspapers, radio and television were given an outline of the Scout Capades by Charles B. Miller Jr., Chairman of the show, at a luncheon held at Pick-Ohio Hotel at the end of October.

Forty business and civic leaders joined the Boy Scout council in planning the huge scout pageant.

Some 1,000 citizens worked on the production which was the first in some 20 years.

The ticket sale drive was launched at a rally October 10th at the Isaly Dairy Company auditorium. Some 175 scout unit chairmen attended. Ticket chairman was Richard Marshall who was secretary/treasurer of the Marshall Mining Company.

Scouts were urged to sell 10,000 tickets. The entire cost of the production was paid for by ticket sales. Awards were made to Scouts selling the most tickets and special commissions were presented to the scout units.

Preparation for this event took over 14 months.

The purpose of the Scout Capades was to show the community the true meaning of Scouting. To acquaint the community with the activities of their Boy Scouts. To show the different phases of Scouting. And to show what Scouting is in the life of a boy.

A 50 piece scout band, opened the Scout Capades to the beat of a brisk march while participating Scouts marched into the field house filling the floor. Director of the band was Lewis Anderson who was band director at Rayen School.

Many acts went on simultaneously on the field house floor. The show was like a circus, but instead of three rings to watch, visitors had dozens of acts to watch at once.

The show was directed by Kenneth Stawn, district council executive at that time.

Events included Cub Scout activities such as playing make believe cowboys and Indians, acting out the Knights of old, playing pirates, doing a space man and Martian skit.

Boy Scouts demonstrated their skills which included first aid, lifesaving, hiking, camping, fire building cooking, and semaphore signaling from towers they built. There were 484 Scouts whooping it up in an Indian dance and a bicycle drill of 50 mounted Scouts.

Explorer Scouts showed their programs of service and social activities.

The story of Scouting was narrated during the Scout Capades as a background while Scouts performed on the floor of the field house arena. At one end of the field house an actor depicted William D. Boyce, a Chicago newspaper publisher, who was credited with introducing Scouting to America. A Boy Scout played the unknown English Scout who "found" the lost Boyce in a foggy London and introduced him to Lord Baden Powell, founder of Scouting.

Also participating was the 32 voice St. Patrick Parish Troop 10 campfire choir directed by Ursuline Sister M. Cecilia.

Cub Pack 94, of the Campbell Christian Center was in an act called "men from mars". On Saturday, November 8th, three of the "men of mars" Cub Scouts appeared on the "Major Ted" TV show at WKBN.

The climax of the show was when all Scouts set up an actual camp with tents, signal towers, cooking fires, and all to demonstrate skills and activities of "A Day at Camp Stambaugh".

Ted Niemi, announcer and director of special events for WKBN Broadcasting Corporation's radio and television, narrated for the Scout Capades.

Over 8,000 spectators showed up for the three day event.

There were over 30 newspaper articles leading up to the Scout spectacular, to promote the Scout Capades.

The General Fireproofing Company's November 1958 News issue featured the Scout Capades with a scout sketched on its cover and five pages inside devoted to Scouting and its history in Youngstown.

SCOUT LEADERS CLUB. On October 3, 1925, a meeting of all Scout leaders of the city was held at which W.S. Hogg presided. Plans were made to form a Scout Leaders Club.

A committee was appointed to submit a constitution and bylaws. H.R. Hartzell, N.H. Jebejian, Joseph Wheeler, H.M. Burk, W.J. Laws, and Chief Harry Hunter were original members of the committee.

First officers were Herbert Hartzell as president of the club, A.G. Magutre as first vice president, N.H. Jebejian as second vice president, John Schiarb as secretary, and H.M. Burk as treasurer.

Men who served as club president later were: E.P. Gilronan, John Schiarb, J.H. Bradfute, W.H. Cook, Oscar Dahlstrom, W.S. Hogg, and Mark Perkins.

In 1930, the Scouter cabin was built by the Scout Leaders Club for Scout leaders use only. Later in 1930 the first council roundtable meeting was held in the Scouter cabin.

SCOUTER CABIN. The Scouter cabin was built in 1930 during the depression by a group of volunteer Scouters known as the "Scout Leaders Club". Some of the members of the club who helped build the cabin were: Club President Oscar Dahlstrom, A.D. Hamilton, Harry A. Walker, Homer Matthews, Bill Hogg, Earl Timlin, and Cy Firth.

The cabin was erected for meetings, social get-togethers, and the enjoyment of all Scout leaders.

Construction of the Scouter cabin was from donated and scrap materials that were scrounged, from nails to the glass for the windows.

No camping was permitted in the cabin the first few years.

The first council roundtable meeting was held in the Scouter cabin in 1930. And early day Silver Beaver Awards were presented to participants in this cabin.

By 1951 the cabin was being used by troop committees, commissioners, and other Scout leader groups. It was equipped to serve light refreshments for up to 24 Scouters, and it had six cots and mattresses for leaders to camp overnight.

Later, the cabin was used for unit camping. In 1967, the original porch was removed, and in 1974, the Scouter cabin was razed due to decay.

SCOUTMASTER AWARD OF MERIT. Two Scoutmasters have received the coveted Scoutmaster Award of Merit. They are Ed Enterline and Ray Slaven.

Ray Slaven, Scoutmaster of Troop 44 in Poland, received his award May 15, 1989. He was honored for 27 years of service as Scoutmaster since 1962 and for celebrating his 85th Eagle Scout Court of Honor under his leadership. The troop also was celebrating its 100th Eagle Scout since its beginning. The Eagle Scout who was honored that evening was Art Volpini.

SCOUTMASTER'S KEY AWARD. A five year training program for Scouters, leading to the "Scoutmaster's Key Award" was adopted by National Council in 1928.

The first training course under that system was held in our council in the spring of 1929 and continued with other sessions each spring and fall.

The first three men to receive the Scoutmaster's Key Award from Mahoning Valley Council were: Norman Ellis, Robert Neeper, and Earl H. Timblin.

SCOUT-O-RAMA. In 1961, the first Scout-O-Rama in ten years was held at Idora Park ballroom on the weekend of November 17-18.

The Scout Rally showed a large number of Scouts taking part in activities that built good citizenship.

The program included performances by a 40 member Scout band known as the "Thunderbirds" under the direction of Lewis Anderson who was band director of Rayen School and James Fitzer who was vocal director at Hubbard Schools.

Numerous displays showed Scout projects such as model rockets, first aid, Braille printing, camping, communications and work in other fields.

In 1971, over 10,000 attended the Scout-O-Rama sponsored by the Boardman Kiwanis Club at the Canfield Fairgrounds May 15-16.

Forty-six Cub, Boy, and Explorer Scouts and leaders numbering 2,000 displayed skills in over 65 display booths and seven exhibit areas to the public.

On Sunday afternoon more than 5,000 filled the grandstands for the harness races. Proceeds from the race benefit youth activities of the Boardman Kiwanis Club which sponsors the event. There was no wagering.

Sky divers from the Alliance Sport Parachute Club thrilled the crowd by landing on the racetrack in front of the grandstand.

State Senator Harry Meshel presented trophies to the winners of the Pine Box Derby Race. The three winners out of 2,500 Cub Scouts were Perry Chickonoski of Pack 101, Jeff Tobey of Pack 112, and Doug Mansfield of Pack 47.

Other Scout-O-Ramas were held in following years.

SCOUTS WORKED WITH FARMING. One hundred Boy Scouts ages 13 and 14 helped with harvesting on farms during the summer of 1943. They helped with the bean, potato, sweet corn, and apple crops. Few of them had previous farm experience but they were "husky boys with a great deal of enthusiasm", Council Executive K.L. Brown said.

Some of the boys stayed on the farms where they worked instead of going home each evening.

The program was arranged by K.L. Brown and Superintendent of Schools at Berlin Center R.H. Ward. He was representative in the county farm agents office.

This was during World War II and many of the Scouts were active in defense work during the summer. The older boys were in the mills while the younger ones were holding less essential jobs.

SEBRING TIMES. In three issues of the "Sebring Times", Violet McNatt (wife of Henry) from Beloit, wrote articles on Camp Stambaugh. They were published on the front cover of each issue. Those issues were:

Thursdays, May 3, 10, 17, 1979.

SILVER BEAVER AWARD. In 1931, the National Council authorized the "Silver Beaver" award for distinguished service to boyhood. This award was to be awarded to men with an outstanding record.

The first four recipients of this award in our council were in the next year, 1932.

Mahoning Valley Council had a confidential permanent committee of three Scouters working on Silver Beaver awards.

In 1955, G. Taylor Evans, during his term as Council President, convinced the executive board to make the Silver Beaver committee a committee of five Scouters. In addition to enlarging the committee the board also made it a rotating committee. Evans appointed the first committee of five. One man was to serve for one year, one man for two years, one man for three years, one man for four years and one man for five years. The Scouter in his final year on the committee, was designated the chairman of the committee. Each year as one man went off the committee, the council president appointed another. When the Scouter went on the committee, he agreed to serve the five years. It was also with the understanding that in his fifth year he would be chairman and then would be off the committee.

SILVER BEAVERS	
1932	Lloyd R. Wallis
	W.S. Hogg
	Herbert R. Hartzell
	Myron Wick
1933	Norman Ellis
1934	W.E. Slagle
	Sidney Moyer
	James B. Jones
	Homer Mathews
1936	E.P. Gilronan
	Joseph Wallace
1937	Horace Yates
	A.G. Maguire
1939	Warren Host
1940	Paul Wick
1941	Robert A. Manchester
	Dr. A.C. Tidd
	Emil Rauschenbach
1942	Less Lee
	Robert Neeper
1943	C. Shallenberger
	Ray Dodson
	Harry M. Burk
1944	Robert H. Holmes
	Harley Ransey
	Cy Firth
	Ray Raub
1945	Frank Bertch
	C.R. Hevener
	A.W. Reigelman
	Ernest Hixon
1946	Harry A. Walker
	James McMaster
1947	T.W. Paine
	Hugh Erskine
	Wilbur Dimit
1948	J.H. Frankle
	Ronald Alexander
	Roy D. Brace
1949	A.D. Hamilton
	Robert Lohrman
	G. Taylor Evans
	Warren Backman
1950	Rev. Robert Uphoff
	James Gustinell

1951	William Bowser
	Hillard Bell
	James Sweeney
1952	M.M. Malmer
	Walter Chuck
	Arnold Stambaugh
1953	David Woods
1954	Peter Zubal
	Gus Arp
1955	James Buchanan
	Arthur Waldo
1956	Martin Z. Bentley
	H.B. Gould
	Robert R. Young
1957	Wayne Stoyer
	William Storey
	Leonard Panella
1958	J.Paul Harvey
	Don Garrett
	Francis Bechenbach
1959	James L. Beeghly
	Herman West
	Mathew Johnson
	Rev. John Hess
	Carl A. Pritchard
1960	Harry Hunter
	James Lawrence
	Henry McNatt
1961	George Woodman
	Ralph Smith
	Carl Pritchard
1962	Robert Renner
	David E. Carroll
	Myron Ferguson
	Fred Gurney
1963	Jesse Gathright
	Frank Steffens
	Marvin Traxler
1964	Barclay Brandmiller
	Henry McNicholas
	E.R. McCleary
	Richard P. Shorts
1965	William Van Dykman
	Edward Cook
	John Wallis
1966	Tom Richardson
	Fred Coombs
	Maynard Ebert
1967	Mylio Kraja
	Jack Sullivan
	Al Schrecingost
1968	Leo Poulakos
	Judge Fred H. Bailey
	Howard Cooper
1969	Jay C. Brownlee
	Walter Payne
	John D. Wolboldt
1970	Paul Hobe
	Aaron Richards
	Philip Stratford
1971	Harry Shagrin, Jr.
	Howard Sherman
	James L. Wick, Jr.
	Louise Price-Fawn
	(First Silver Fawn Recipient)
1972	Seymour I. Fewer
	Samuel Lores
	Martin Wendt
	Hilda Sherman-Fawn
1973	J. Robert LaCelle
	Ray E. Slaven
	Rev. A. Swinehart
	Betty Davison-Fawn
1974	James S. Houser
	Murle L. McLaughlin

	Chester W. Taylor
	Georgia Grimm-Fawn
1975	Michael Balaban
	Jack D. Brammer
	Edwin K. Enterline
1976	Don M. Johnson
	Judge John J. Leskovansky
	Ida L. Magee
1977	Russell L. Bunger
	John B. Kundracik
	Viola Wayne
1978	Theodore Gavozzi
	Charles H. Kneen
	Janette Ruse
1979	Robert Davis
	Ronald Gedra
	Charles Lee
1980	Donald G. Baumgartner
	Corrine L. Lawson
	Donald L. Ruse
1981	John P. Moyer
	Harry T. Pancher
1982	Louis Chicchillo
	Marvin M. Tradler
1983	Paul Luke
	Byron W. (Bud) Harnishfeger
1984	Rudolph C. Barth
	Anthony Castranova
	William G. Lyden, Jr.
1985	Harland (Bud) Mattison
	Alex M. Seka
	Earl W. Yost
1986	Anna R. Wheller
	Stephen F. Seifert
1987	Dallas T. Heston
	Henry Sforza
1988	Michael Dyer
	Joseph R. Novotny
	Michael H. Russell
1989	John A. Gustafson
	Andrew M. Wheeler
1990	Tony Valley,Jr.
	Richard Hart
1991	Joe Eighan
	Anthony Vivo
1992	Martin Gilboy
	Richard Cook
	Don Hall

1993 .... (not available at time of printing this book)

SPRUCE TRIANGLE. The Spruce Triangle is located in camp between the swimming pool and the Katschke cabin. Spruce trees in the shape of a triangle, around a grassy area, make up the Spruce Triangle.

It's not known when the trees were planted to form the triangle, but early photographs suggest the triangle was planted in camp during the 1920s.

During the summer camp season, Scouts would quietly leave the last council fire of their week in camp to file into the Spruce Triangle. On their way across the creek from the council fire ring they picked up a rock from the creek bed. When they arrived in the triangle, they added their rock to the pile of rocks that were previously placed there by other campers.

These rocks represented each Scout and Scouter from each year who attended summer camp. The rock pile meant to serve as a lasting memory of all the friendships formed at camp.

Henry Katschke brought this idea to Stambaugh when he became our Council Executive in 1949. This program existed for twenty years until 1969 when the large rock pile was removed because of snakes living in it.

STAMBAUGH, HENRY H. On January 4, 1919, Henry H.

Stambaugh at the age of 60, died of unknown causes. Ill health was expected. He was a well respected community leader who was very much interested in the Boy Scout program in Youngstown.

In Stambaugh's will, he left his farm that was located on Leffingwell Road in Canfield, to the Boy Scouts of Youngstown. The farm contained 86½ acres and became known as the "Stambaugh Scout Reservation". Phillip J. Thompson was named trustee of the camp in the Stambaugh will. Stambaugh and Thompson were business partners in the Stambaugh-Thompson Company.

Henry H. Stambaugh was born November 21, 1858 in Brier Hill near Girard. He died a bachelor in 1919 while on business in New Orleans. He was the son of John Stambaugh and Caroline Hamilton Stambaugh. The Stambaugh Municipal Golf Course and Stambaugh Auditorium were named in honor of Henry H. Stambaugh.

Henry attended Youngstown public schools until age 17. He then attended Greylock Institute in Williamstown, Massachusetts before going to Cornell University for two years.

He left Cornell in 1879 to work for Brier Hill Iron and Coal Company in manual labor. The company was founded by David Tod in 1859 as president. Followed later by John Stambaugh, Henry's father. Joseph G. Butler, Jr. was manager.

John Stambaugh was a partner and one of the pioneer iron makers of the valley. He and David Tod were involved in some of the earliest ventures in the industry here in Mahoning Valley.

Henry H. Stambaugh was with the company from 1879 to 1912 in the following capacities: a laborer, secretary, treasurer, and finally as president.

The business had grown and prospered. Henry owned large coal fields in Pennsylvania and valuable iron ore mines in Michigan. By 1912, Henry was president and chairman of the board of the Brier Hill Iron and Coal Company. His company merged with others into the Brier Hill Steel Company. The merging companies were: Brier Hill Iron and Coal, Youngstown Steel, Thomas Steel of Niles, and Empire Iron and Steel of Niles.

Henry had many other business interests. He was director of many corporations. He was deliberate in his judgment, and firm in his conviction. He was considerate and sympathetic, but forceful in all his dealings with men. He was by nature, philanthropic.

Henry was very interested in nature and rural life. He loved dogs and horses. Much of his recreation was on the three large farms he owned. Two farms in Mahoning County and one in Trumbull County.

Later in life he gave much time attempting to better the conditions of those less fortunate. He held faith in human nature. His charities, both public and private, were large. He gave more liberally to worthy causes than any other man in the Mahoning Valley. His giving was done in a quiet manner. Few knew the extent of his generosity.

He was intensely patriotic. He helped government financing during the great war, and helped needy families of our own soldiers, widows and orphans of France and Belgium.

He left a large portion of his fortune to five trustees for the purpose of building in the city of Youngstown and the Mahoning Valley. His counsel was frequently sought by leaders in finance and industry. He held directorships in the Youngstown Sheet and Tube Company, First National and Dollar Banks, the Tod-Stambaugh Company, and the Bessemer Limestone Company. He was one of the promoters and builders of the Stambaugh building. He helped organize the Realty Guarantee and Trust Company. He actively identified with every movement in Youngstown for community betterment, lending not only his moral support, but his financial assistance most generously.

He controlled extensive realty holdings in Youngstown. He had a small herd of Jersey breed cattle on his farm in Canfield which became the Stambaugh Scout Reservation.

He lived for many years in the Stambaugh homestead on Belmont Avenue opposite St. Elizabeth's Hospital. Relatives include brothers John Jr. and George Stambaugh, and a sister Mrs. Fred Wilkerson.

He had a retiring nature, disliking public attention. He was modest and performed his many deeds of benevolence in a very quiet manner. He played an important part in developing the Iron and Steel industry of the Mahoning Valley.

He left two-thirds of his fortune, estimated at three million dollars (keep in mind that this was in 1919) to his friends, charitable and philanthropic enterprises. Not a dollar of his estate was created by the loss of a dollar by another person.

Among the educational enterprises which he endowed, was a fund for a high school. Seven hundred and fifty thousand dollars for the erection of an institution for the scientific and technical training of the community.

He believed that all labor, mental and physical, should have a just return. He said, "... the greatest help that could be offered mankind, was the increase of opportunity".

Henry H. Stambaugh was regarded as Youngstown's most influential citizen.

STAMBAUGH EMBLEM. Even though the Stambaugh Reservation began operation as a Scout camp in 1919, it wasn't until the year of 1950 that the council adopted an emblem for the reservation which also became the summer camp emblem.

The camping committee very carefully set about to make this an emblem that would be worn proudly. It was not to be just handed to anyone.

It was decided by the camping committee and approved by the executive board that all Scouts and leaders would have an opportunity to earn the emblem. There were only two requirements: (1) Ten days and nights of camping at Stambaugh, and (2) Ten hours of service to Stambaugh.

In the emblem's early years, a record card was provided for each man and boy to keep his own record. Troop or council records were not kept in connection with the program. When the card was properly filled out, it was turned in to the camp director. Then, through proper ceremony in the Spruce Triangle, the emblem was awarded Friday night. No record was kept of those who earned the emblem. It was not to be traded to anyone for any reason. If a Scout or leader lost his, he could purchase another. The program revolved around the honor system.

The ceremony for awarding the emblem remained in the hands of the camp director. On occasion, the camp director would authorize the program director to perform the ceremony.

THE EMBLEM

"The emblem says the wearer is a good camper.

The imperfect 'triangular shape' of the emblem reminds us that the reservation will never be perfect and only through our efforts will it improve. The person who has earned the emblem agrees to always try to improve the Stambaugh Scout Reservation by keeping it clean or by participating in a major improvement project.

The 'star' reminds us that God has given us a beautiful place and we must preserve it.

The 'crescent' represents the moon that was sacred to the Indians. Many of the traditions at Stambaugh are of Indian tradition or legend.

The 'inner triangle' is a symbol of the whole council. The 'green background' of the emblem reminds us to keep young Scouts coming to the reservation so it can continue to exist.

The 'red' represents the blood of our body that caused our hands to be red from the hard work we perform on the reservation.

The 'gold', a precious metal that carries with it high standards, reminds us to keep our own standards high."

Some time after the Stambaugh Emblem was adopted, the Spruce Triangle became a restricted area in camp. Only those who earned the Stambaugh Emblem were permitted to walk into the sacred ground of the Spruce Triangle. But during the 1980s this custom was no longer enforced.

STAMBAUGH MEDAL. After the development of the Stambaugh Emblem in 1950, the council through the camping committee also established the plan to train Senior Patrol Leaders. This training took place in the week prior to the week the S.P.L.'s own troop was in camp. The majority of S.P.L.s did earn the medal.

The requirements were kept simple: (1) The S.P.L. had to attend the program planning session with his scoutmaster. (2) The S.P.L. had to attend the training program for the full time in the period preceding the period his troop is in camp. (3) The S.P.L. had to do a satisfactory job in the training period. (4) The S.P.L.'s boys had to follow him and his troop leaders had to allow him to perform as a Senior Patrol Leader.

If these requirements were met, the Stambaugh Medal was pinned on the S.P.L.'s uniform by the camp program director at the final retreat ceremony in the period of camp in which his troop was camping.

The requirements were strictly adhered to in the earlier days. The Scouts who earned the medal wore it proudly. It had come to mean much in designating the young man as a leader.

The council bought the medals from the Balfour Company before the Boy Scouts of America National Supply Service went into the jewelry business.

STAMBAUGH TRIBE OF GOOD INDIANS. This program was started in the 1930s by Harry Walker. Each camper would try to earn a beanie (skullcap).

Different progress levels were indicated by colored beanies. Brown, "Papoose"; maroon, "Pathfinder"; green, "Runner"; and blue, "Hunter"., The purple was for "Brave" which was awarded to the campers for leadership.

Tribe council meetings were always held after bedtime on Friday evenings. The Scouts who were to receive awards were awakened in their bunks and led to the "Secret Council Ring" by one of the leaders. The secret council ring is believed to have been in the area where the Elm campsite is today.

The ceremony was very impressive. They were performed by leaders who wore dye on their bodies to make them look like an Indian. There was a central council fire and then four fires surrounding it, manned by four Indians who gave inspirational messages during the ceremony.

At the conclusion of the ceremony, the chief would ascend a hill with a blazing torch and speak inspirational words to the assembled Scouts and leaders.

STAMBAUGH'S GRAVE. For many years since 1919, a pilgrimage was made to the grave of Henry Stambaugh in Oak Hill Cemetery. Each year this marked the closing of Boy Scout anniversary week.

Almost the entire membership of the Boy Scouts of Youngstown made the annual pilgrimage each February in the cold and snow. They started at Scout headquarters which was at the Reuben-McMillan Library at Wick and Rayen Avenues. They paraded down Wick Avenue, through town, and up Market Street lead by the local Scout Drum and Bugle Corps.

Once at the grave site, prayer was offered, a wreath was placed on Mr. Stambaugh's grave by the latest recipient of the Eagle rank, the Scout prayer was sung, and taps played. Then the parade reassembled and marched from the cemetery.

STAMBOREE. At the "Stamboree" which opened the summer camping season in 1931, two prominent men in National Scouting visited Youngstown.

One was Eagle Scout Paul Siple of Erie, Pennsylvania who talked on his experience as a Sea Scout in the Antarctic with Admiral Richard Byrd. The other was Bunnar H. Berg of the National staff who was director of volunteer training.

STATUE OF LIBERTY REPLICA. In New York City, the colossal Statue of Liberty sits on an island in New York Harbor. It was erected there in 1886, a gift from France to the United States. It is the symbol of American freedom and American opportunity.

At the Mahoning Valley Council Scouting Exposition in April of 1951, Scouts revealed plans to erect a ten foot copper replica of the Statue of Liberty.

Then on Flag Day, June 14th, the statue replica was unveiled in Wick Park. The next day the statue was moved to a permanent location at the corner of Wick Avenue and Wood Street were it faced Wick Avenue.

It was set on a concrete base. To the right of the statue was the Rayen School of Engineering on the Youngstown University Campus. Behind the statue was the Board of Education building.

It was one of a number of replicas placed throughout the nation that year by various participating councils, as part of Scouting's 40th Anniversary. The national theme was "Strengthen the Arm of Liberty".

In her right hand was a bronze tablet engraved "July 4, 1776" in Roman numerals. A bronze plaque on the base of the pedestal read, in part, "The Boy Scouts of America dedicate this copy of the Statue of Liberty as a pledge of everlasting fidelity and loyalty."

Scouts and other interested people purchased "shares" to finance the $300 project. They were called "shares of liberty" and were sold for as little as 25¢ a share. Those who purchased a share received a colorful certificate. Robert Renner was chairman of the statue committee.

Troops shared in the maintenance of the statue after it was erected since the pigeons frequently visited it.

The pedestal was designed by P. Arthur D'Orazio and William Pesa, local contractors at that time.

At the Annual Recognition Dinner in March of 1952, at the Calvin Center, J.D. Fowler, president of the J.D. Fowler Company was presented a miniature Statue of Liberty because his company erected the Statue of Liberty.

The statue remained in view for 14 years, and then it was stolen. No police report was ever made. It is believed to have disappeared on a week-end sometime in the spring of 1965. It was never recovered.

One man recalled, "She was there on a Friday, and Monday she was gone".

It is possible that Liberty was melted down for sale? Or is she hidden beneath years of dust in an attic, garage, or maybe a fraternity or sorority house? Who knows?

In 1976, Council Executive Ted Parker looked into the possibility of replacing the statue. But the foundry in New Jersey that cast those statues no longer existed.

STOCKADE PROGRAM. Around 1931, summer camp had program divided into areas known as stockades. Campers slept in tents on wooden platforms and were arranged in a semicircle. The stockade director and assistant shared a smaller tent opposite the camper's tents. Each tent had four double-deck bunks to hold eight boys. Straw filled sacks were used for mattresses. Later when camp resorted to strictly troop camping, where each unit provided its own leaders, preparing its own food, etc., semipermanent buildings were constructed in each camp area which served as a food preparation building.

The SEA LION STOCKADE was located near the waterfront (lake). It was for First Class Scouts only. The program included the following merit badges: Swimming, Lifesaving, Canoeing, Personal Health, Public Health, Athletics, and Physical Development. Also included were: Scout Life Guard, Junior and Senior Red Cross training. Fun activities included: water sports, athletic meets, treasure hunts, campfires, stories, songs, games and canoeing.

In 1931, Eagle Scout Arthur Thomas of Troop 15 from South High School was the "Head Sea Lion" (director) and Donald Perry was the "Assistant Sea Lion". Perry was an Eagle Scout from Troop 4 and Rayen High School.

The DAN BOONE STOCKADE was for 1st Class Scouts only. The program included the following merit badges: Bird Study, Reptiles, Insect Life, Weather, Leaf Printing, Conservation, Signaling, Forestry, Photography, First Aid, Public Health, Personal Health, Athletics, and Physical Development. Fun activities included water sports, camp fires, canoeing, stories, athletic meets, games, treasure hunts, and songs.

In 1931, Eagle Scout Louis M. Voyer was "Head Dan Boone". He was from Troop 9 and Rayen High School. "Assistant Dan Boone" was Mark Gunlefinger Jr. He was an Eagle Scout from Troop 19 and Rayen High School.

The AIRPORT STOCKADE and KIT CARSON STOCKADE was located in the flat area around the Hunter cabin. This stockade was for 1st and 2nd year campers. Program included first aid, signaling, tracking, pace, swimming, map making, judging, knife and hatchet, fire building, cooking, compass, safety, 14 mile hike, axemanship, and nature study. Fun activities included campfires, athletic meets, games water sports, stories, treasure hunts, special handicraft projects, songs and canoeing.

In 1931, "Stockade Airport Commander" was Eagle Scout Joseph Hafkenshiel of Troop 28 and Rayen High School. "Assistant Airport Commander" was Eagle Scout Clarence Covington of Troop 54 and South High School. He became Attorney Covington. He was also Henderson and Covington Law Firm in Youngstown.

"Head Kit Carson" was Eagle Scout John Bakody of Troop 9 and of Rayen High School. "Assistant Kit Carson" was Eagle Scout Alonzo Jacque of Troop 53 and of Rayen High School.

The FORESTER STOCKADE was located on the flat up the hill behind the old chapel. This was an exclusive group consisting of experienced campers who had to be 1st class and second year campers or equivalent. Program included the following merit badges: Archery, Basketry, Pioneering, Camping, Leathercraft, Leatherwork, Cooking, Carpentry, Wood Carving, and Wood Work. Specialties included axe throwing, archery, golf, and rope making. Fun activities included camp fires, songs, games, athletics, swimming, canoeing, and treasure hunts.

In 1931, "Head Forester" was Eagle Scout Roger S. Kimberly of Troop 36 and Grove City College. "Assistant Forester" was Eagle Scout Ralph Barner

of Troop 54 and from South High School.

STROUSS CABIN. The Strouss cabin was built in 1947 from a log cabin kit as part of the capital fund campaign of 1946 camp improvement projects. Clarence Strouss Sr. provided the necessary funds.

The cabin was named in memory of Executive Board member Isaac Strouss.

In 1953, the cabin's foundation had to be rebuilt due to decay of the joists, some flooring and log siding from water run-off down the hill behind the cabin. Also a roofed front porch was added. Then in 1986, the cement block foundation collapsed from the earth's shifting down hill. This took place inches every year until the cabin was left without support.

SUSTAINING MEMBERSHIP ENROLLMENT (S.M.E.). Sometime in the year of 1966, Council President J.C. Brownlee, Finance Chairman Henry McNicholas, and Council Executive Henry Katschke, attended the first conference on Sustaining Membership Enrollment at Schiff Scout Reservation in New Jersey. The information gathered at the conference was of great value.

After returning from the conference, the first attempt at executing the S.M.E. program was taken in our council. In the following year of 1967, three times more money was received. And by 1968 the program was well established, better understood, and being done openly.

With development of a strong S.M.E. program by 1968, the council proved to everyone that they were able to secure the funds needed to finance the operating program as well as the long range plan.

The S.M.E. program is still used by our council today.

SWANSTON PROPERTY. In January of 1985, Mahoning Valley Council purchased 270.63 acres of land known as the Swanston property for $440,000.00. The land is adjacent west of Camp Stambaugh and extends to Raccoon Road.

The original Stambaugh acreage of 86.5 acres was willed as a gift to the Youngstown Boy Scouts in 1919 by Henry H. Stambaugh after his death. Rocco Marino gave 28.5 more acres in June of 1946.

In order to pay for the $440,000.00 debt incurred in the purchase of the Swanston land, the executive committee decided to sell lots along Leffingwell and Raccoon roads for housing only. Twenty-two lots were plotted averaging two acres each totaling 47.63 acres. This reduced the usable acreage for camping in the new property from 270.63 acres to approximately 223 acres. This brought the total acreage for Camp Stambaugh to 338 acres.

First: the sell of lots along the perimeter of camp provided income to help pay the $440,000.00 property cost. Second: the sell of perimeter lots provides a buffer area between camp property and street access.

A two-story, six-room farm house located on Raccoon road on the Swanston property was refurbished. Camp Ranger Ross Lucarell and his family reside in the house.

Mr. William Swanston, a retired farmer, died in 1919. He stipulated in his will that a portion of his substantial estate be used to establish and maintain a home on his farm for Mahoning County's poor and disadvantaged children. Mr. Swanston said several times in the original will, "use my land". Mr. Swanston had great concern for youth.

In December of 1978, trustees of the Swanston estate tried to alter Mr. Swanston's will due to the lack of building funds for such a home. In 1979, the Children's Services Board didn't think Mr. Swanston's land would be suitable to establish the facility.

The years moved on. Taxes and other pressure regarding the Swanston land caused the Swanston estate trustees to channel the property usage, as close as possible, to the intent of the will.

In filing suit, the trustees asked the court's permission to sell the property to purchase land closer to the city of Youngstown and build a children's home there.

A portion of the land was used in the late 1940s for a Christ Mission Camp.

Between the 1960s and January 1985, when our council purchased the property, the Swanston estate trustees allowed use of the land for the Boy Scout's inner city program, and Cub Scout Summer Day Camp Program.

SWIMMING POOL. The camp swimming pool was built by the Rotary Club of Youngstown and dedicated September 11th, 1963. It was placed in full service for the 1964 summer camp season.

The Rotary Club sponsored an annual horse show produced by the Mahoning Saddle & Bridle Club at the Canfield Fairgounds. Net proceeds from the shows went into the swimming pool project.

The pool was placed in full service for the 1964 summer camp season. Water to fill the pool was pumped from Indian Lake.

The pool is 75 feet in length, 55 feet wide at the shallow end and 35 feet wide at the deep end. The pool holds 120,000 gallons of water.

Total cost was $65,000. This included the pool, filtration system, the original pool heater which was never fired up and later sold, showers, dressing rooms, toilet facilities and washing facilities.

The final payment of $20,761 for the pool was made in December of 1967.

(1) Henry H. Stambaugh. He gave his Canfield farm to the Boy Scouts in 1919. (2) William T. Storey, Council President, 1964-1965. (3) Jack Sullivan, 1967. Scoutmaster of Troop 6. (4) Frank K. Stillwagon, Council President, 1968-1969. (5) Sulfur spring drinking fountain near Indian Creek below the dam, 1930. Scout on left holds his nose because of the strong sulfur smell. (6) Kit Carson Stockade campsite, circa 1920. (7) Members of the Scout Leaders Club edging slabs for the Scouter cabin, 1930. From left: A.D. Hamilton, Harry Walker, and Bill Hogg. (8) Building the Scouter cabin in 1930. (9) Scouter cabin in 1949 with original porch. (10) Strouss cabin as it looked when built in 1947. (11) The shower house in 1955. It was located between the Wick Lodge (not shown) to the left and the Dining Hall (not shown) to the right. The horizontal pipe at right carried hot water from the dining hall. (12) Inside of the shower house, 1955. (13) Boy Scouts honoring the memory of Henry Stambaugh on the 17th National Anniversary of Scouting in February of 1927. Front row from left: Mike Malmer with U.S. flag, Keith Clupper with B.S.A. flag, William Campbell with third flag, next five unknown, Carlyle Thomas with first bugle, next two unknown, Adrian Dignan fourth bugler. Placing the wreath on the grave of Henry Stambaugh is Michael Bogan from Troop 43 in Struthers.

Photo credits: 1,6,8 authors collection; 2,3 photos by Lee Banks; 4 (Vindicator, pg 5, 1/31/68); 13 (Vindicator, Gravure, 2/27/27); 5 16mm movie film; 7,9 A.D. Hamilton album; 10 (1950) photo by Henry Katschke; 11,12 Spratt Studio.

(1) Schwebel Memorial Lodge, 1965. (2) Members of the Schwebel family during the dedication of the Schwebel Memorial Lodge on Friday, September 24, 1965. Shown are from left: Mrs. Frances Greenberger, Mrs. Sadie Rifkin, Executive Board member J.H. Frankle, Dave Schwebel, Mrs. Elaine Winick, and Irving Schwebel. (3) A day at Camp Stambaugh is demonstrated to visitors at the Scout Capades in 1958 at the Struthers Field House. (4) "Scout Week" window display in 1955 at McKelveys department store in downtown Youngstown. (5) Paul Siple, a Scout from Erie Pennsylvania, reported on a trip he took to the South Pole with the famed Admiral Byrd at a Scout meeting in Youngstown in 1936. (6) Dedication of the pool September 11, 1963. Pictured in front of the filter house are (standing from left): Rotary President Guion Osborn, past Rotary President Dr. Eugene Beech, Mahoning Valley Council Vice-President Richard Shorts, (seated) General Chairman for the pool project Attorney Robert M. Hammond, and past Council President G. Taylor Evans.

Photo credits: 1,2,3, photos by Lee Banks; 4 authors collection; 5,6 Vindicator.

TAYLOR, BENNET D. Bennet Taylor was Assistant Council Executive of our council from March 15, 1969 until he retired the end of December in 1977.

Bennet is a native of Bourbon County in Kentucky where he joined the Lone Scouts as a boy. He served as Scoutmaster for three years in Mt. Vernon Ohio. In 1941 he began his professional Scouting career as a Field Executive at Hamilton Ohio.

From March 1943 to April 1946 he served in the U.S. Army as an officer in the Infantry Rifle Company where he earned 13 awards and decorations.

After release from the Army, Bennet served as District Executive at Logan West Virginia from 1946-1948, Council Executive at Bowling Green Kentucky from 1948-1952, Assistant Council Executive at Springfield Ohio from 1952-1959, Council Executive at Columbiana Council in Lisbon Ohio from 1959 to 1969, and Assistant Council Executive of Mahoning Valley Council from 1959-1977.

In 1968, Kentucky Governor Louie Nunn appointed Bennet Taylor a Kentucky Colonel. Bennet is an ordained Deacon in the Presbyterian Church and retired Lt. Colonel from the United States Army.

While in Hamilton Ohio, Bennet worked in Scouting with Paul Siple from the Miami University faculty in Oxford Ohio. Paul Siple was a Scout selected in 1928 to be part of the crew in the Admiral Richard Byrd Expedition to the South Pole.

Jere Ratcliffe became Chief Scout Executive of the National Boy Scouts of America in 1993. Bennet Taylor was his camp director in the 1950s.

TELESCOPE IN CAMP. In the summer of 1926, The Stambaugh Scout Reservation received 1 of 6 ten inch telescopes in the city made by T.G. Beede. A small cabin known as the telescope cabin was built to store the telescope and a thick pipe base, that still exists today, was cemented in the ground to support the telescope. It was placed at the top of the hill in camp where the Emil Rauschenbach Flag Pole is today. The cabin was later used by the O.A. and razed October 1987.

It all began in 1922. W.S. Hogg who worked with Scouting and was a friend of Mr. Beede, asked Mr. Beede if he would make a telescope for the Scout camp. Mr. Beede said that he would try. In 1922 telescopes were not available as today.

From the time Mr. Beede was a boy he had always wanted to see what the Milky Way and the star clusters of the sky were made of. So it became the great ambition of his life to make a perfect telescope. In 1898 he read an article written by Reverend John Peate about the method of building telescopes. Reverend Peate was a retired pastor from Pittsburgh and a telescope making enthusiast now living in Youngstown.

On July 4, 1898, Mr. Beede went to visit Reverend Peate. The reverend showed Mr. Beede the principles involved and the actual tools used to make a telescope.

John Brashear was one of Reverend Peate's Parishioners in Pittsburgh. Brashear was a pillar in the community and one of America's greatest telescope makers. Brashear and Peate talked over astronomy together from time to time and Peate's interest grew finally learning the expertise from Brashear on how to make telescopes.

Mr. Beede, through months of experimenting, was able to make his first lens in 1900. It was a 5-3/4" crude lens but he could see the mountains

of the moon, the rings of Saturn, and the lettering on a wind mill six miles away.

In 1910 when Haley's comet was here, he had just completed his first twelve inch lens which he displayed at his home on Hillman Street.

Thousands of Youngstown citizens looked at the sky through Mr. Beede's telescope. After returning home from a hard day at work he would spend hours showing others his telescope. This was his great childhood ambition, and he accomplished it.

In 1926, a ten inch telescope, which was under construction intermittently since 1922, was ready for installation at the Scout camp.

The telescope was dedicated at the opening of summer camp in June 1926 with speeches from W.S. Hogg, Council Executive Myron C. Wick, Mr. T.G. Beede, Dr. C.C. Booth who helped finance the project, and Council Commissioner John Chase. There were 500 Scouts and parents present with a flag ceremony and bugle calls.

Mr. Irvine Marshall was in charge of the telescope. During summer camp he showed Scouts the stars, one stockade group at a time.

Later on, the telescope was used for astronomy merit badge classes. The Astronomy Club of Youngstown instructed.

TEN YEAR GROWTH PROGRAM. In 1933, President Herbert Hoover offered an award to each troop that reached certain standards in the "Ten Year Growth Program" adopted by national headquarters in 1932. The slogan was "One out of every four new male citizens, a four year Scout trained man". This recognition was received by 41 local troops.

THOMPSON, PHILLIP JACOB. Thompson was council executive from 1914-1918. He was president of the Stambaugh-Thompson Company that was owned by Thompson and Henry Stambaugh. Henry Stambaugh selected Thompson as trustee of the Stambaugh farm for use by the Youngstown Scout program.

Thompson was in charge of the "Court Of Honor" which tested Scouts for awards. The examinations were held in the Stambaugh-Thompson Company on West Federal Street. Thompson also directed the first Scoutmaster school in our council.

He was a great administrator who attracted community leaders who were experts in their field to serve as Scout examiners. He also had an influence on the financially able.

TRAINING CENTER. In 1982, the training center was built in Camp Stambaugh on part of the previous parking lot. It was a community service project of the Boardman Rotary Club. Mahoning County Joint Vocational School did the carpentry. Scouters have named it the "Rotary Building". Cost of construction totaled $78,000.

TROOP 23. The following is from an interview with John Wallis December 1987 who was in his early 80s. He joined Troop 23 at age 10 and later as an adult served on the Council Executive Committee.

"Most of the boys in Troop 23 were from the Sunday School class of Mr. R.C. McBride, who became the Scoutmaster. When the Troop started in 1913, the original group of 12 boys met at the Richard Brown Memorial Church at Elm Street and Woodbine Avenue on Friday evenings.

At that time the Boy Scout movement was very loosely operated. New troops were on their own. Fortunately a First Class Scout from another troop later joined Troop 23 and became very useful in helping others through their tests.

One of the first activities of a new troop was to go camping. A campsite on the McBride homestead on the Grand River near West Farmington, Ohio was selected.

The troop took the B&O Railroad from downtown Youngstown which had a stop at West Farmington. Scoutmaster McBride's father would have his hay wagon with a team of horses waiting to carry the gear. The Scouts hiked about two miles to the campsite.

After making camp near the bend in the river, the Scouts built a dam by placing sand bags between a fallen tree and the river floor to make the water deep enough to swim in. We camped there for two weeks each year until 1918 when the council had its first council camp.

Equipment and supplies of all kinds had to be improvised. A large tent to hold everyone was procured. Each Scout brought a large empty cloth bag to be filled with straw for his bed. He brought his own table service, pillow and blanket. He also had to bring $1.50 to pay for his food for the week. It was a requirement that the $1.50 had to be earned.

Once at the campsite, an outdoor stove was built of bricks. All meals were cooked over an open fire by Mrs. McBride on the first couple of campouts. A long table and benches were built on the site. Because the Grand River was only about three feet deep, the Scouts wedged sandbags between some big trees that fell across the water and the river floor to form a dam.

Fresh milk each morning came from a nearby farm. Milk in a tight can lowered into the cool river supplied refrigeration. Parents and guests brought food donations. A crate of oranges brought by Mrs. Felton on the first campout was greatly enjoyed.

Mr. McBride tried to commute in his "Tin Lizzy" from his work to camp. It was a difficult task at that time over the rutted, dusty country roads, not much like the good country roads today.

In 1914 we put on a play called "Up Caesar's Creek" at our church and other churches in the area in order to make money for our campouts. We were able to get a larger tent, we had books and Homer Williams gave us a Gramophone to use. We brought it on our campouts.

In 1915 and 1916, we brought the Hiawatha Indian Company to Mill Creek Park to put on the 'Hiawatha Pageant'. Real Indians performed for two weeks both years. We made enough money to rent better tents and equipment for the troop.

We now had a lady cook. We found a wood-burning stove that we got working for our campsite and allowed us to have home made pies and cakes at camp. A real treat for all of us.

Our camp was well established by this time. The boys did more Scout work and advancement. Our camp fires were becoming more enjoyable and everyone was happy.

By 1917 the troop was so used to camping that the whole camp could be set up in 45 minutes. Emergencies such as tents collapsing in heavy rain and the like were taken in stride. At this time the troop was actively engaged in selling war bonds, appearing in parades, and helping in other civic affairs. The troop had grown into a very closely-knit group.

John Chase was council commissioner and was always ready to lend his assistance in nature hikes. With the growth of the Scout movement and many Scout troops, a full time commissioner

was engaged and council camping was organized. All troops in the council were required to attend camp.

This Scouting experience as a young boy now only lives on as a memory."

(1) Troop 23, circa 1913. 1st row (from left): Billy Black, unknown, Charles McBride Jr. 2nd row: unknown, Red Green, Dean Roberts, unknown, Bill Hunt, unknown, 3rd row: unknown, Bradley Williams, Scoutmaster Charlie McBride, unknown, Bob Hearn. Top row: unknown, unknown, Henry Hedges. (John Wallis album). (2) Myron Roberts reading Boys Life Magazine in 1914. This photo was published in a later issue of Boys Life Magazine. He was not of scout age but tagged along with his brother who was in troop 23. Myron became president of Mahoning National Bank. (John Wallis album). (3) The ten inch telescope made for Camp Stambaugh by T.G. Beede in 1926. (photo by Youngstown Arc Engraving Co). (4) The telescope stand, 1987. K.L. Brown Pavilion in background. (photo by author). (5) Troop 65 Scouts, totally or partially blind, use Braille machines to show their independence. The troop was sponsored by Youngstown Society of the Blind. From left: Barry Stirbens, Louis Kolman (counselor), Ronald Kolman, and Anthony Aeras. (Vindicator, November 1961). (6) Raven Patrol of Troop 21 from St. Mathias Church, circa 1940s. Front row (from left): Robert Martinko, Joe Sagula, Cyril Hudak. Second row: Joe Reduga, John Sagula, Joe Hudak. Back row: Mike Yanek, Bob Lilko, John Leskovyansky, Ed Palatas, Frank Novotny. (Judge John Leskovyansky album). (7) Troop 23, 1914 at the West Farmington troop camp enjoying the Gramophone. John Wallis (interviewed) is fourth from right. (John Wallis album). (8) Training Center in Camp Stambaugh known to the Scouters as the Rotary Building. (photo by author, 1985). (9) Troop 9, June 1913, on an 80 mile hike to the Clarion River Forest Company in Pennsylvania near what is known today as Cook Forest State Park. The horse and buggy was used to carry gear. Troop 9 was sponsored by the First Presbyterian Church beginning in 1912.

WALKER, HARRY A. Harry Walker was known to all as "Ranger Walker". He was born in Canada, worked here as a structural iron worker, and loved the outdoors and his fellow man. He was always with a smile on his face. He was a natural leader and hard worker.

Harry Walker became interested in Scouting in 1919 when he joined up with Troop 17 at Science Hill. The troop was weak then. But under his leadership as Scoutmaster, it became one of the leading troops in the council.

Early in 1922, Walker gave full time to Scouting for a life's career. He was appointed field executive and caretaker of the Stambaugh Scout Reservation.

Harry and his wife lived on the Stambaugh Reservation in the farm house from 1922-1945 when they moved to Canfield. They had a total of ten children by previous marriages, six boys and four girls. All ten children were reared in the tradition of Scouting. All they knew was "Boy Scouts". Six grandchildren became Scouts.

Harry organized the Northeast, Southwest, and Suburban districts in the council. In 1945 he was in charge of the Hubbard and Eastern divisions.

The Scouts knew that you didn't earn Pioneering Merit Badge from Harry by building models. He insisted that you cut trees, trim, drag them to the site, and lash them together with rope. No shortcuts were allowed. Harry was that way with everything.

At the 1945 annual council meeting in the Y.M.C.A., Walker was honored for his fine work and commitment to Scouting.

On March 31, 1945, Harry Walker retired as camp ranger and assistant council executive. He continued working in Scouting as a volunteer. He also served as Justice of the Peace in Canfield Township.

He died at age 93 in 1972.

WALKER CABIN. The Walker cabin was built during the camp improvement project in 1947. It was constructed from a log cabin kit that was identical to the Strouss cabin. The Walker cabin was named in honor of Ranger Harry Walker.

The clearing in front of the Walker cabin, known as the Walker area, served as the central gathering place for many campwide activities and training courses, while the Walker cabin served as headquarters.

Behind the Walker cabin at the bottom of the hill was an outcropping of coal. This coal was dug out and brought up the hill with a horse and wagon along a road that led down to the coal area from the Beech Knob campsite. Harry Walker would stay in the back room of the Chief's Lodge (later known as Katschke Lodge) on the week-ends and sold coal to the Scouts by the bucket for the outdoor kitchen stoves and for heat in the cabins during the winter.

WALLIS MEMORIAL LODGE. The Lloyd R. Wallis Memorial Lodge was dedicated in August, 1965. It was donated by Mrs. Lloyd Wallis and family and originally intended to be used as a program planning center for Scout Leaders. It has served as a winter camping cabin and a summer nature lodge.

Lloyd R. Wallis died January 1, 1962. From the beginning of Camp Stambaugh in 1919, he was among the early Scouters of our council who gave leadership to the development of Stambaugh and was the first chairman of the Camp Stambaugh Camping Committee in 1919 and council vice-president in 1913. He was a Scouter of great vision.

WALNUT CABIN. Its been told by several Scouters that a shack was found floating down Indian Creek and was added on to the back of the Walnut cabin. This was around the 1930s or 1940s.

The Walnut cabin was originally built in the same place and facing the same direction as the Moyer Health Lodge. The Moyer Health Lodge replaced the Walnut cabin July 1967.

In July of 1953, the Walnut cabin was remodeled. During the 1960s, it was used as a summer camp office and a weekend ranger's station in the off-season.

WHITE BIRCH CAMPSITE. Behind the Wick Lodge during the 1930s and early 1940s was a campsite called the White Birch Campsite.

WICK, JAMES L. Jr. James L. Wick was council president in 1918. In the Youngstown Historical Society you can find notes he wrote on the beginning of Youngstown Council.

He invited Ernest Thompson Seton to lecture in Youngstown. Seton was one of two originators of the Boy Scouts of America. Daniel Carter Beard was the other originator.

At age 28, James Wick served as council treasurer from 1911-1915.

WICK LODGE. The Wick Lodge was built in 1932 in memory of Myron C. Wick Jr. Myron Wick died in 1930 at age 38. He was council president from 1925-1929. A gift of cash from the estate of Myron Wick Jr. was provided for maintenance of the building.

His picture is still displayed over the fireplace in the Wick Lodge as it was when the lodge was built.

One story told was that when the Wick Lodge was built in 1932, it was a simple one floor building made of four sides and an "A" frame roof and in 1946, the roof of the lodge was raised in order to add the upper three rooms. But earlier photographs disprove this story.

Whenever the upper section was built, the only access to it was from a front upper level porch with steps located on the west end of the porch.

In the late 1940s the kitchen and toilet room were added to the back side of the building. The only access to the toilet room was from the outside around back of the lodge.

Harry Walker built the original cupboards in the kitchen and paneled the inside of the main room with wormy chestnut wood that still exists on the walls today. The kitchen has a small basement under it that extends under the rest rooms for access to the water pipes. The basement is accessible from inside the kitchen through a trap door under one of the cabinets.

In 1955, another room was added to the back west corner of the lodge. This room provided storage space and inside access to the toilet room.

In 1964, Paul Wick and his sister Mrs. Newell C. Bolton, contributed funds to repair the lodge. The front deck, upper porch and steps were removed due to decay. Early in 1965, new stairs accessing the upper level rooms were built on the outer back side of the lodge. The front doorways for the three separate rooms on the second floor were moved to the back side of the rooms to gain access from the back steps. Windows replaced the front doors on the upper level rooms and individual roofs and porches were built over lower level doors. Extensive work was also performed inside the lodge.

In the late 1970s, another outside stairway to the upper level was built on the back west side of the building to replace the decayed back steps. In the early 1980s, a stair way was built inside the main room through the floor to the upper level rooms. Prior to this time, each room was separate. When the inside stair way was built, a doorway cut from room to room was opened.

The Wick Lodge was used for training courses and leaders meetings. During summer camp season, senior staff members lived in the upper section. In 1951 the council made the Wick Lodge available for groups outside of Scouting at a charge of $5.00. The Wick Lodge had a capacity of 60 people. In the late 1960s and in 1990 and 1991, the Wick was used as the summer camp office

In the late 1960s, Troop 7 of St. Anthony's church in Briar Hill used it for mass services during their annual father and son winter campout.

WICK PARK CAMPOREES. The first in town Boy Scout camporee took place on a week end in Wick Park in June of 1943. Tents, rustic cooking stoves and other hand made facilities sprang up within hours.

About 200 Scouts camped in Wick Park which is located on the north side of town near the Stambaugh Auditorium. The Scouts representing 15 troops and forming 27 patrols, pitched camp in an orderly, efficient manner. They provided their own primitive refrigeration.

Scouts began arriving in the morning, by bicycle, on foot and by bus, some pulling their own trailers by hand, with all equipment they needed for the two day campout.

By 3:00pm the usually quiet park looked quite cozy.

The sea patrol, in sailor outfits, camped near a water pump with a rope fence around their area. A sentry pacing up and down changed duty with another Scout every two hours. They were in charge of the water. Another group built a signal tower of rope and branches several feet tall, and climbed up and down it after it was built. Others built rustic racks for their towels, and mountings for wash basins.

One patrol was prepared even for mosquito attack with citronella scenting the air for yards around.

The Cub Scouts were there too, just during the day, with their displays. They were too young to camp out and were merely observing. They were eager to tell what they were doing, as all the Scouts were.

Scouts weren't without an audience, as children from the nearby neighborhood lined up around each individual encampment and watched wide eyed.

Some participating adults in charge were: Council Executive K.L. Brown, director of the camporee James V. Hanley, assistant directors Ben Pelleschi and Kenneth Ward, Health and Safety Director Robert Young and his assistant Joseph E. Collins, in charge of first aid was E. Timblin, Activities Director Leland Clegg and his assistant J.J. Friedland, in charge of records was Horace Beggs and Hugh Erskine, Chief Observer Cy Firth assisted by Claire Hevener, Warren Host, Al Reigelman, Dale Wegele, Ted Vorkape, Bob Loheman, Nick Huber and Lloyd Lindemer.

A special feature of the Scout camporee in Wick Park in June of 1943 was the dedication of an ornamental fireplace in memory of John H. Chase, playground director, who was a naturalist and friend of boys.

H.M. Van Arsdale with the help of several Scouts, constructed a memorial fireplace built of stones brought and erected by the Scouts.

Sidney Moyer, representing the Scouts, made the presentation, and the fireplace was formally accepted by the city through Charles A. Leedy, vice-chairman of the City Park and Playground Commission.

A tablet on the fireplace read, "Erected by Boy Scouts of Mahoning Valley Council in memory of their friend, John H. Chase."

In 1945, about 305 Youngstown District Boy Scouts from 39 troops attended the third annual Mahoning Valley Boy Scout Camporee in Wick Park which ran from Friday noon, June 7 to Sunday night, June 9.

"Attendance was 50 percent higher than the previous year", Council Executive K.L. Brown said.

Scoutmaster of Poland Troop 44 Dale Wegele directed the camporee. He was assisted by Camping and Activities Chairman of the Struthers-Lowellville District F.A. McNeil, vice-chairman of the same district Robert Young, Council Advancement Chairman E.P. Gilronan, Field Commissioner of Senior Scouting Cyril Firth, Scoutmaster of Troop 24 Andrew Debrosky Jr., Scoutmaster of Troop 14 Earl Hazel, Executive Board Member H.M. Burk, and Scoutmaster of Troop 19 William Greenberg.

Friday's program included a camp inspection at 2:30pm by Scoutmasters and troop committeemen, flag raising and flag lowering ceremonies and a camp fire program at 9:00pm. Field Executive R.B. Major was master of ceremonies. Some 600 parents and friends of the Scouts were guests at the campfire.

Patrols participated Saturday in first aid demonstrations, exhibitions of Scoutcraft, tent pitching, compass games, fire building, signaling, knot tying, egg boiling, and stalking tests.

Each Scout received a ribbon bar award at a special ceremony Saturday night for satisfactory participation in the camporee.

The camporee was a preliminary outing for summer camp. Summer camp operated June 25 through August 27 at the Stambaugh Reservation that year.

Also held in Wick Park by Scouts was a Wick Park Rally on May 11, 1957, and a winter campout on February 11, 1961.

WILSON, DAVID H. Dave Wilson was assistant council executive in the late 1960s.

He died January 18, 1969 from a heart attack. He was participating in a winter weekend outing in Camp Stambaugh and upon feeling tired and weak, he went home to rest and passed away.

WOOD BADGE. The pioneers of Scouting realized that Scout leaders must be trained. The highest level of training available for adult leaders in Scouting is Wood Badge training. It is Scouting's premier training course.

Wood Badge started in 1919 by Baden Powell at the International Center of Scout Leader Training at the Scout reservation in Gilwell Park, England. The symbol of Wood Badge training is two little beads hung on a boot lace. The two beads are copies of those taken from a necklace which General Baden Powell captured from Chief Dinizulu during his African encounter in 1887. This is how the training course was named Wood Badge, because its symbol was literally a badge of wood.

Gilwell Park Scout reservation in England was the gift of W. DuBois MacLaren in 1919. The Gilwell neckerchief displays the tartan of the clan MacLaren. A woggle made of leather is used as a neckerchief slide for the Gilwell neckerchief. The ax and log is the camp emblem or "totem" of Gilwell.

Lord Baden Powell directed the first Wood Badge training course in 1919 at Gilwell England and gave each of the participants one of the beads which he had captured from Chief Dinizulu.

The first Americanized Wood Badge training course took place at the Schiff Scout reservation in New Jersey from July 31-August 8, 1948. William Hillcourt, better known as "Green Bar Bill" directed this first Wood Badge course.

OUR FIRST WOOD BADGE COURSE

Mahoning Valley Council hosted its first and only Wood Badge course, EC-390, August 20-27, 1989 in Camp Stambaugh. There was a total of ten staff members and twenty-three participants from Ohio, Michigan, and Pennsylvania representing the following ten councils: Bucktail (BTC), Buckeye (BC), Greater

Cleveland (GCC), Detroit Area (DAC), Dan Beard (DBC), Firelands Area (FAC), Mahoning Valley (MVC), Northeast Ohio (NOC), Western Reserve (WRC).

In 1987, I went to Council Executive Fred Baird and the executive board to see if I could interest them in having Mahoning Valley Council host its first Wood Badge course. Its an expensive and time consuming venture, but the council agreed to do it.

Our application to host a week-long Wood Badge course was accepted by the region and I was asked to serve as the course director.

I invited "Green Bar Bill" Hillcourt as our guest. A year of correspondence took place between Hillcourt and I. Since he usually attends functions that draw large crowds, he was reluctant to accept my invitation. But I convinced him to attend.

In Hillcourt's speech during the "feast", which is a great supper of foods cooked by patrols at the end of the course, he gave his reason why he accepted the invitation. He said, "I decided to come here because, you are the first Scoutmaster of the first Wood Badge course in this council, and I was the first Scoutmaster of the first Wood Badge course in the United States."

Many people pulled together including friends, Scouters, and community business people to make EC-390 Wood Badge course a success in Mahoning Valley Council.

MAHONING VALLEY COUNCIL WOOD BADGERS

James Alexander	Bill Moss
Upton Anderson	John Nash Jr.
Fred Baird	Harold Norton
Mike Balaban	Harry Pancher
Kenneth Barnes	James Parker
Don Bechdolt	Ted Parker
Jack Bokesch	Carlisle Pritchard
Bill Colyer Sr.	Bob Puhalla
Rich Cook Sr.	Dave Rhodes
J.H. Cooper	Stu Rila
Larry DeCamp	Dick Robart
Jim Driscoll Sr.	Bob Roberts
Glen Duncan	Joseph Roble
Bradley Dutton	Don Ruse
Joseph Dutton	Jerry Rushton
Jeff Dyer	Al Schrecengost
Bob Eisen	Steve Seifert
Wilfred Eisenbraun	Henry Sforza
Ed Enterline	Dale Shaffer
Dan Fink	Howard Sherman
Wally Fowles	Ray Slaven
Ron Gedra	Bill Stilson
Rob Gingery	John Stroney
H. Gorby	Ginger Sullenger
Ron Harris	Jack Sullivan
Bud Harnishfeger	Elaine Susany
Melvin Hoffman	Betty Taucher
John Holderman	Joe Taucher
Jim Houser	Chet Taylor
Bill Hunt Sr.	Marvin Tradler
Joe Johnson Sr.	Tony Valley Jr.
Donna Kascsak	Bill VanDykman
George Kascsak	Don VanNess
Harold Kasten	Art Waldo
Denny Keslar	Viola Wayne
Chuck Kneen	George Weamer
Mike Kupec	Harold Whagoner Sr.
Dr. John LeBrun	Andy Wheeler
Ida Magee	John Wilkinson
Don Majors	John Williams
Earl McCleery	Bob Wilson
Murle McLaughlin	John Wolboldt
Tom Miller	Georgianna Zellinsky
Cecil Monroe	
Ken Moore	

WORLD JAMBOREES, 1920-1959. 1st, 1920, London, England. Baden Powell was acclaimed, "Chief Scout of the World". Held indoors. 2nd, 1924, Copenhagen, Denmark. Held indoors, camping. 3rd, 1929, Birkenhead, England. Considered as the "Coming Of Age Jamboree". King George V honored Baden Powell as "Lord Baden Powell of Gilwell". Eleven Scouts and leaders from Youngstown Council attended. 4th, 1933, in Hungry. 5th, 1937, in Holland. Baden Powell gave his "Closing Message". 6th, 1947, France. 7th, 1951, Australia. 8th, 1955, Canada. First Jamboree outside of Europe. Considered, "The Jamboree Of New Horizons". 9th, 1957, Birmingham, England. Considered, "Jubilee Jamboree". Held in England to celebrate 100th birthday of Baden Powell. 10th, 1959, Philippines. Others followed.

WORLD WAR I. On July 28th, 1914, World War I began. The United States declared war on Germany April 6th, 1917. This brought the United States into World War I. This war involved every continent on the globe and more than 9/10 of the population of the world. The full resources of the Boy Scouts of America were placed at the service of the government under the slogan of "Help Win The War". The Youngstown Council limited all Scout service for the duration of the war to government needs.

With a sense of duty to God and Country, Scouts all over America were responsible for the sale of millions of dollars of Liberty War Bonds and War Savings Stamps to help finance the war.

Following a request from President Woodrow Wilson, Scouts all over the country took part in a survey of woodlands to locate black walnut trees which were needed in the manufacturing of airplane propellers. Scouts also collected 100 train car loads of fruit pits which were used in gas masks.

Youngstown area Scouts developed "Scout Acres" where they planted War Gardens to help feed the soldiers. The message was short but meaningful: "Every Scout to feed a Soldier. You will need one hoe, 75 cents worth of seeds, a Scout's will, a strong arm and a heart full of patriotism".

The Youngstown Liberty War Bond campaign was held October 20-25, 1917. There was a Liberty Loan Parade with the Fife & Drum Corps. Ohio Governor Cox, invited our Scouts to raise the Liberty Loan flag. The top Liberty Bonds salesman was Scout Ritter Levinson of Troop #19.

The war ended in 1918.

(1) William Hillcourt, "Green Bar Bill", (left) was a guest at the only Wood Badge training course hosted by Mahoning Valley Council, August 1989. Tony Valley (right) was course director. (2) EC-390 Wood Badge Staff, 1989. Front row (from left): C/C Dan Fink MVC, C/C Jeff Dyer MVC, C/C Ray Dargis CLC, C/C Denny Keslar MVC. Back row: Quartermaster Jack Bokesch MVC, Senior Patrol Leader Skip Reigel CLC, Committee Chairman Bart Pragnell BUC, Scoutmaster/Course Director Tony Valley MVC, Assistant Scoutmaster Ray Slaven MVC, Assistant Quartermaster Jim Dade WRC. Not pictured: Course Advisor George Swain NEC. (3) EC-390 Beaver Patrol. Front: Jack Sullivan WRC PP, Roland Waller CLC. Back: C/C Dan Fink MVC, Ray Leatherberry BUC, Ken Moore MVC, Dave Jones DBC. (4) EC-390 Bobwhite Patrol. Front: Scott McWilliams CLC, Glen Duncan MVC, Henry Sforza MVC. Back: C/C Ray Dargis CLC, Dolores Sullivan WRC, Don Neubert BTC PP, John Palo WRC. (5) EC-390 Eagle Patrol. Front: Tim Grosswiler FAC, Doris Fitzgerald WRC, Joe Rossi WRC. Back: C/C Denny Keslar MVC, Dave Turpin BUC, Rich Cook MVC, Paul Frank DAC PP. (6) EC-390 Fox Patrol. Front: Joe Taucher MVC, Bob Wilson MVC, Ed Luhn DBC. Back: C/C Jeff Dyer, Dan Dade WRC, John King WRC, Ron Harris MVC PP. (photos 1-7 by Jack Acri). (7) Camp Ranger Harry Walker, 1959. (8) Myron C. Wick Jr, circa 1926. Was council president 1925-1929. The Wick Lodge was built in honor of him.

Abbreviations Used Above	
BTC-Bucktail Council	FAC-Firelands Area Council
BUT-Buckeye Council	MVC-Mahoning Valley Council
CLC-Cleveland Council	NEO-Northeast Ohio Council
DAC-Detroit Area Council	WRC-Western Reserve Council
DBC-Dan Beard Council	C/C-Coach/Counselor
	PP-Permanent Patrol Leader

(1) Wick Lodge, circa 1950. (2) Wick Lodge among the tall pines, winter circa 1978. Used for Christmas card by author. (3) Inside the Wick Lodge at the retirement party of Council Executive K.L. Brown in 1949. From left: Incoming Council Executive Henry Katschke, Mrs. & Mr. K.L. Brown, unknown, retired Council Executive Harry Hunter, and unknown. Portrait of Myron C. Wick on wall in background. (4) Wick Park Scout Camporee, circa 1943. (5) John Wallis, 1965. (6) George Woodman, 1966. (7) Council President David E. Carroll (right) presents the presidents trophy to Arrowhead District. From left: District Chairman G.T. Wick, District Executive Dave Wilson, District Commissioner Ed Cook, 1962. (8) The Walker cabin, 1947. (9) Scouts ages 13 and 14 in 1947 from Troop #45, Mahoning Methodist Church, getting ready to ride their sled down the hill behind the Walker cabin. From left: Bob Edle, Bill Adsit, Walter Jennings, Ron Gedra and Fred Gault. (10-11) Walnut cabin before and after remodeling, 1953. (12) Wallis Memorial Lodge, 1965. (13) Washstand with running water used in the 1950s and 1960s. (14) Viola Wayne (center), 1966. (15) Marty Wendt (right) goes over Summer Camp program in 1959 with the Senior Patrol Leader of Troop #13.

Photo credits: 1,10 by Spratt Studio; 2 by author; 5,6,12,13,14,15 by Lee Banks; 7 by Vindicator; 9 Ron Gedra album; 3,4,8,11 author's collection.

75

SECTION IV

photo by Jack Acri

Frederick L. Baird
Council Executive

"As I Remember 1970-1993"
by Council Executive Fred Baird

"AS I REMEMBER 1970-1993"

an autobiography by

Fred Baird
Council Executive, 1985-1993

In June of 1970, I was drawn to professional Scouting primarily because I felt Scouting was doing the best job of impacting young people for good.

Bart Ingram, who was Council Program Director then, had a great deal to do with my decision. As I was entering professional Scouting, I had no way of knowing that at the same time the movement was undergoing major changes under the banner of BOY POWER. Almost immediately I realized that Scouting was having upper management problems that were driving professionals away by the hundreds. I too would have left the profession had it not been for Bennett Taylor who was Assistant Council Executive. He took me under his wing and gave guidance through several rough years.

In spite of the lack-luster first few years, I enjoyed my job as District Executive of Pioneer District from 1970-1975. Part of my territory included less affluent areas of the council which presented many unique challenges. The job was accomplished even though there was very little money and too few volunteers.

I developed the program "In School Scouting" with cooperation of the Youngstown Board of Education. This program was designed to promote Scouting in the inner city schools by meeting once a week after school in one of the classrooms where a 45 minute Scout meeting was held. This operated for two years. I organized and supervised the para-professional program in our council to help aid the "In School Scouting" program. It was a poor substitute for Scouting, but it was better than nothing.

In 1973, I organized Troop 4 at Butler Memorial Church which shared a common parking lot with the council office on Rayen Avenue. The boys all came from Smoky Hollow, a tough place to grow up. I served as Scoutmaster for three rewarding years.

In November of 1974, Ted Parker who was a member of the National staff, replaced Dean Johnson as Council Executive of Mahoning Valley Council.

In 1974, I coordinated and instructed the first East Central Region "Cub Scout Day Camp" seminar at National Camp School in Kalamazoo, Michigan.

Our council was one of the first councils in the country to run a Cub Scout Day Camp. It was held at Camp Stambaugh in 1974 with 250 Cub Scouts in attendance. I recruited such people as Betty Davis, Barbara Brown, and Viola Wayne to write the materials and conduct the camps. They were done so well that the Boy Scouts of America asked Viola and I to conduct training courses throughout Indiana, Ohio, Michigan and West Virginia.

Council Executive Ted Parker and Council President Russell Bunger gave me approval to negotiate a formal agreement with the Swanston Estate Trustees for the use of Camp Lexington as a Cub Day Camp. The property was adjacent to Camp Stambaugh. By February of 1975 the agreement was reached which included the Swanston Trustees donating $20,000 toward much needed repairs and $4,000 for the first year's program. I used the Joint Vocational School to assist in repairing the camp. We named our new camp, Camp Akela, and hosted about 575 Cub Scouts in 1975 and near 700 in 1976.

Determined to provide a high quality program for the Scouts in Pioneer District, I met with District Chairman Don Davis along with District Activities Co-Chairmen Tony Valley Jr. and Joe Angelo Sr. to create the Outriders in 1975. This unique group of older Scouts from various troops in the district operated as service teams that helped troops in need and they also designed and operated exciting district programs. The program was entirely boy operated for two years with Tony Valley and Joe Angelo serving as adult advisors. And for some reason, we had our own currency as well as several patches made. We were making things happen on the boy level with the boys ideas and boy leadership. We thought we were really making history when a man from the National office visited us to see what we were doing. We were sure we would be featured in Scouting Magazine. Not so! He gave a cease and desist order, on the basis that boys were not permitted to hold adult positions.

By 1976, I was promoted to the position of Program Director, and in 1979 to Assistant Council Executive.

After Columbiana Council Executive Ed Dillon retired in 1980, I accepted that same position. In 1985, Mahoning Valley Council Executive Ted Parker died suddenly. I returned to Mahoning Valley Council as Council Executive in August 1985.

Council consolidation talks between our council and Western Reserve Council in Warren began in 1984. Ted Parker initiated the talks, before his death, due to financial concerns for both councils. The consolidation was voted against by council membership on both sides in 1986.

Thanks to the foresight of the Executive Board under the leadership of Council President Charles Cushwa III and the late Ted Parker, our council purchased the adjoining Swanston property of 270 acres for $440,000 in January of 1985. With a $105,000 short fall in the operating fund, we faced a big challenge. As usual, the volunteers of the Council Executive Board under the leadership of Council President Michael Russell, in 1986, accepted the challenge to always operate in the black. By year-end we were current with all our day-to-day obligations. In two and a half years we had the $440,000 mortgage paid off and had added $75,000 to our Trust Fund. This was accomplished by selling lots for family housing on Leffingwell and Raccoon Roads.

Part of the austere management required reducing the professional staff to one person. (Few councils ever recover from such a move.) Penny Shaffer was hired as Registrar and Trading Post Manager, Nancy Bokesch was hired as the Accounting Specialist and Systems Manager. After about two years, we began to add professional staff. David Dickhoff was added followed shortly by Kenneth Moore. After three years, both David and Kenneth were promoted to larger councils. They were replaced by Erik Lingrin.

In 1989, Harry Pancher introduced me to Robert Neff, Eagle Scout of 1932. Mr. Neff wanted to do something for Scouting. He agreed to provide funding for the much needed camp administration building. He asked that it be called the Eagle Cabin. Also in 1989, the Boardman Rotary Club agreed to build a much needed dining hall at Camp Stambaugh, at an estimated cost of $340,000.

The fall of 1991 will be remembered for BENCHMARK 2000, a strategic plan for the 1990s concerning the way Scouting would do business. The most recognizable impact on local councils is the fact that small councils will be consolidated so as to meet the minimum standards of operation. National was insistent this time that consolidation must take place.

In the spring of 1992, Council President Dr. Michael Woloschak appointed Executive Board members, Joe Leithold and Calvin Stroble to serve with him as representatives to meet with their counterparts from North East Ohio Council in Painesville and Western Reserve Council in Warren for the purpose of exploring the feasibility and desirability of consolidating the three councils. It was determined that consolidation would greatly enhance the Scouting program for all concerned. The three Executive Boards approved the recommendation to consolidate together and placed the matter before the voting body of each council on February 10, 1993. A name for the council has not been chosen at the time of this printing. I feel the most appropriate name was chosen in 1800 when the western portion of the Connecticut Reserve, on the southern shore of Lake Erie, was designated as the "Western Reserve".

Few people enjoy the broad, far reaching opportunities that Professional Scouting has provided me. Many of the Valley's finest people are among my friends and associates, all because of Scouting. Together our energies have prepared thousands of young people to be productive, participating members of society. We were "called" and committed to prepare today's youth for the future". Together we have made a difference in the kinds of adults our young people become.

I'm proud to be a Scout!

COUNCIL OFFICE STAFF, MARCH 1993

1   2   3   4

(1) Erik Lingrin....Senior District Executive.
(2) Nancy Bokesch...Accounting Specialist and Systems Manager.
(3) Penny Shaffer...Registrar and Trading Post Manager.
(4) Ross Lucarell...Camp Ranger.

SECTION V

TONY VALLEY, JR.

Author and Memorabilia
includes: The Story About This Book

In this section, I took the liberty to reminisce. I have had a very rewarding life, with Scouting a large part of it.

Reviewing pictures and slides for this section brought back many wonderful memories. Not only memories of Scout buddies and Scout leaders, but of family and friends who were there throughout the years, and memories of personal achievement.

Joined Troop #7 in 1959

In October of 1959, I joined Boy Scout Troop #7 at St. Anthony's Roman Catholic Church at age 10½. The Briar Hill Church had just moved from West Federal Street to Turin Avenue and first chartered Troop #7 October 31, 1959. I was the second registered member of the newly formed troop, the Scoutmaster's son being the first.

Troop #7 was a well organized and very active unit. Larry Drombetta Sr. was Scoutmaster and committed to the youth of the troop. He had served as a volunteer on the district and council levels in prior years. The troop committee gave full support and participated in the troop operation which guaranteed its success. On a monthly basis we went camping, hiking and toured various places like G.M., Schwebels Bakery, WHOT Radio, and others.

Original committee members were: Chairman Joseph (Pat) Menelle, John Cafaro, Anthony Valley Sr., John Vogrin Sr., Sam Addeo, and Vincent Adduci. In October of 1965, my dad became committee chairman and held that position for 26 years until October 31, 1991.

As the years went on I served in all the patrol and troop leadership positions including Patrol Leader, Senior Patrol Leader, Junior Assistant Scoutmaster, and Assistant Scoutmaster. Since I played trumpet, I seemed to have always been the Troop Bugler as a Scout.

My Scout buddies in the troop were Eugene DeGeorge and John Vogrin Jr. We worked well together planning and carrying out troop activities. We also served on the staff of many district and council events.

In 1967 our Scoutmaster became ill. At age 18, I assumed the Scoutmaster's duties until a replacement could be found. On October 31, 1968, Henry Sforza Sr. became Scoutmaster of Troop #7. Henry held that position for 24 years until October 31, 1992.

I remained registered as Assistant Scoutmaster until 1984 when I registered on the troop committee. During this time, I helped in the troop where needed and mostly worked with the district and council activities. When the troop reorganized in 1991, I registered with the council.

Others who served as Scoutmaster of Troop #7 were Sam Addeo (1962), and John Altieri (1963, 1965-1967).

Awards Earned

On March 11, 1966, I earned the rank of Eagle Scout. I was the first Eagle Scout in Troop #7. The troop held a large dinner ceremony in the school auditorium with the Knights of Dunamis present, of which I became a member. By the time I reached my 18th birthday, I had acquired all three Eagle Palms with a total of 51 merit badges out of the 102 available at that time.

On December 18, 1966, Eugene DeGeorge and I became the first Scouts from Troop #7 to earn the Ad Altari Dei Catholic religious award.

In 1967, I was elected by my troop into the Order of the Arrow, and in 1968, I was elected by the lodge to serve on the Executive Committee as Secretary. In 1969, I was vice-chief. During my term I was in charge of making a book on "how to run an Ordeal". On October 14, 1972, I was awarded the Vigil Honor with the Indian name of "Tye Daka Rih'Hon" which means, The Flying Messenger. From 1971-1973, I was advisor for the lodge newsletter, "The Arrowflight". In 1978 and 1979, I served as Lodge Advisor.

In 1984, the Catholic Committee on Scouting honored me with the Bronze Pelican Award. And in 1990, Mahoning Valley Council honored me with the Silver Beaver Award.

Philmont Treks

My first trip to Philmont Scout Ranch in New Mexico was in the summer of 1972. I was assistant advisor and Jerry Bertin was our crew chief (similar to a patrol leader). Scouts and leaders from our council traveled to Philmont by bus. Jerry and I drove to Philmont in my Toyota Corolla with primer paint blotches all over it. We were seen coming for miles! I enjoyed the 12-day Philmont backpacking adventure so much, I promised myself I'd return with my own crew someday.

On July 9, 1976, I filled my 15-passenger van with 13 Scouts and one other leader and headed west on a 33 day trip to Philmont. National Parks and Monuments visited before arriving at Philmont included: Badlands, Mount Rushmore, Crazy Horse and Black Hills in South Dakota; Yellowstone and Grand Teton in Wyoming; Zion in Utah; Grand Canyon and Petrified Forest in Arizona; and Rocky Mountain National Park in Colorado on the way home. We camped out every night and cooked all our meals over an open fire. A rotating duty roster created by the crew chief guaranteed everybody a responsibility.

I conducted similar trips in 1977, 1978, 1979, and 1980. In 1977, I had three crews travel to Philmont by van. A moment I will never forget on that trip was when all three crews met at the base of the Tooth of Time in Philmont. Each crew was on their own itinerary through Philmont. We had agreed to meet the last day at the base of the Tooth of Time at a set time. As my crew approached the meeting place with Crew Chief Roby VanVlerah in the lead, over one ridge came Advisor Jeff Dyer's crew with Crew Chief Dom Valley (my brother) in the lead, and down the trail came Advisor Dave Adams' crew with Crew Chief Jeff Driscoll in the lead. What a feeling of fellowship and accomplishment we all felt. It was an exciting moment.

To prepare for these trips I conducted monthly training sessions beginning in the fall of the previous year of the trip. Parents were required to attend the first three sessions with their son in order to learn about the trip, equipment needed, and to gain their support. At least two week-end training trips took place. Since map and compass was part of my training session, I created a book titled, "Topographic Maps and The Compass, can be easy and fun" in 1977. As it turned out, over 5,000 books were printed and sold to outdoor outfitters in several states and to Philmont Scout Ranch. One of the R.O.T.C. instructors at Youngstown State University used the book in his training courses because it was much simpler to understand.

In 1985, my good friend Ray Slaven who was Scoutmaster of Troop #44 in Poland, asked me to work with his troop chairman, Bill Colyer in planning a trip to Philmont in 1986 via commercial airline to and from New Mexico. We did just that. It was such a great time, we did it again in 1988!

Wood Badge Experience

On March 23, 1976, I received my Wood Badge beads after attending EC-76 which was a week long training course at Camp Butler in Akron September 6-13, 1975.

Having a strong desire to serve on a Wood Badge staff, I constantly stayed in contact with a couple of staff people from EC-76. Finally, my persistence paid off. I was invited to serve on staff as a Coach/Counselor for EC-109W. This was a week-end course held at Camp Beaumont in Cleveland, May and June of 1977, Bill Starn was Course Director.

Other Wood Badge courses that I served on staff of were: EC-144, as Senior Patrol Leader at Camp Stigwandish in Painseville, August 12-19, 1978, George Swain was Course Director; EC-330W, as Assistant Senior Patrol Leader at Camp Butler in Akron, August and September weekends, 1986, Don Wiseman was Course Director; EC-334, as Quarter Master at Camp Stigwandish in Painesville, August 8-15, 1987, George Swain was Course Director; SE-472, as Coach/Counselor at Camp Callaway in Columbus, Georgia, April and May weekends, 1988, Bart Ingram was Course Director; and finally EC-390, as Scoutmaster at our council camp, Camp Stambaugh, August 20-27, 1989, I was Course Director. EC-390 was the first and only Wood Badge course hosted by Mahoning Valley Council.

Other Experiences

In 1991 and 1992, I served on the East Central Region National Camping School Aquatic Training Staff. The school was held both years at Anthony Wayne Scout Reservation in Pleasant Lake, Indiana.

From 1986-1991, I was an active member of the Council Executive Board.

Since 1966 I've spent many years on summer camp staff at Camp Stambaugh. I've been the camp clerk, bugler, nature director, fieldsports director, lakefront director, aquatics director, inner city Scouts director, and camp program director.

At age 22 in 1971, I was Camp Director for our council's "Big Oak Wilderness Camp" in Highlandtown, Ohio. The program theme was wilderness adventure. Council Camping Director Bart Ingram designed and supervised the program. Scouts backpacked everything in to and out of their outpost campsites either on foot or on trail bikes.

I had four outpost staff. My brother Nick Valley taught orienteering and astronomy studies, Ken Goist taught wilderness survival skills and edible plants, Jerry Evanoff taught campcraft skills, and Scott Callahan taught hunter safety and skeet shooting.

In 1974 I was program director at Camp Stambaugh when after two weeks, Council Executive Dean Johnson asked me to be the Camp Director, of which I accepted. Then in late April of 1990, Council Executive Fred Baird asked if I would be Camp Director for Stambaugh because the man they had, resigned. I met with Fred to discuss this matter and found that nothing had been done to prepare for the 1990 season. It seemed like a challenge to me so I accepted the position. I had to find a program director, staff, cook, and order supplies and food. Plus, attend National Camping School for a week to be certified.

Thanks to the full cooperation of Council Executive Fred Baird, Camp Ranger Ross Lucarell, Program Director Mark Hradil, my Aunt Clara Casale who accepted to be the camp cook, and many other devoted camp staff, we had a very successful summer camp. In fact, we all did it again in 1991!

Through-out the years, I've had the pleasure of working with many fine Scouts and Scouters of which new friendships were made. And just like any other person active in Scouting, I somehow couldn't say no when asked to take charge of something. Some other programs that I directed at one time or another were: Catholic Committee on Scouting's Father Kane Camp, district and council camporees, training courses and roundtables.

Life Is About The Journey You Take

I wrote on Page 1 of this book, "Life is not about accomplishments, Life is about the journey you take along the way". I have acted upon many opportunities in my life that have led me on many journeys. One must prepare themselves for opportunity, so when it comes, they can recognize it and know what to do.

As a follower, I've learned from those who led, accepting the qualities that interest me, trusting and challenging along the way, but always maintaining my own journey.

As a leader, I've learned that my success in leadership resulted because of the trust and loyalty of those who followed.

My parents were very active and committed to the Scouting program. Both of my younger brothers, Nick and Dom, received their Eagle Award and my only sister, Mari Ann Valley Cann, was active in the Girl Scout program. Her daughter Jennifer is a Girl Scout and progressing very well.

Out of literally thousands of people that I have come to know throughout the years, there are several who have a special place in my heart; part of the reason for this is their unquestionable trust, loyalty and sincerity, ...they know who they are.

The Story About This Book

I have remained registered with the Boy Scouts of America since first joining in 1959. After taking a three year break from working as a volunteer on the district and council levels, I became active again in 1984. Upon my return, some of my cherished friends of all ages had either moved away, retired from Scouting or passed on to the great Scoutmaster in the sky. It disturbed me that new Scouts and new leaders didn't know anything about their predecessors or some of the great events of our council's past. So I decided to compile some historic facts. I began researching, interviewing and writing which nine years later resulted in the completion of this book. Ironically, the two subjects in school I did poorly in were History and English!

After several years of research and interviews, I investigated professional book printing services. My intent was to have a book with hard cover, glossy paper, over 800 large photos and over 200 pages. But the cost to produce such a book was beyond my means. Most printers required a minimum of 1,000 books printed. All the production including typesetting, screening photographs, layout, printing, and hard cover binding was quoted to cost over $16,000.

Wanting the best quality book, I made an effort to raise the money. I went looking for pre-paid book orders. Council Executive Fred Baird was very cooperative. We mailed a flyer advertising the book. Out of the 2,000 registered Scouts and Scouters in the council we mailed to, plus newspaper articles in the Vindicator, Tribune and area township papers, less than 65 people responded! Seventy-five grants relating to history preservation were applied for resulting with a response of 100% "NO"!

Then Council Executive Fred Baird brought this project to the Council Finance Committee for support. The council was in no financial position to finance the book.

As a last attempt to raise money, I asked over 1,000 area businesses to "adopt a book for a library".

These books were to be donated to area libraries with the donors name on the inside cover. Libraries were to include public libraries, school libraries, hospital and other area libraries. Only the following five businesses responded: Valley Tool and Supply Company, c/o Lane A. Cornell, 1 book; Hardee's Restaurants, c/o Syl Frazzini, 1 book; Gail & Jill McCullough, 2 books; The Feed Bin, c/o Eleanor Mort, 1 book; and Mikel's Party Shop, c/o Eagle Scout Mike Metcalf, 1 book. Individuals who sponsored a book for a library are: Leonard Paskevich, 2 books; William Hunt family, 1 book; and Ed Cook (in Arizona) 1 book. The result was much less than I expected.

The decision to go ahead with this project became a financial problem. Because of the delay in publication, several people asked for refunds. In fact, several were quite verbal in demanding their money back. Refunds were made lessening funds available for printing the book.

I had no choice but to cut printing costs drastically or abort the project. From the 2,000 photographs of historic value that I collected since beginning this project in 1984, about 800 were selected for the book. But due to cost cuts, less than 200 were used in this book. Instead of having the text professionally typeset, I typed it at home. By reducing the size of the photos and text, the amount of pages required were also reduced. I did the layout work at home, cutting and pasting everything together, making the book camera ready for printing. The book was, however, printed on acid free/archival quality paper. Needless to say, I was very busy at a hard task of scaling down the book!

These production cuts brought the cost down, but not enough to meet the expenses. So my dear mom and dad, determined to see this work in print, contributed the needed money to complete this book.

It was a long unmarked trail to the completion of this work. Countless hours were spent on this project over the past nine years.

Two newspapers were researched, the "Telegram" and the "Vindicator". Both have been transferred to microfilm in the Reuben-McMillan Library on Wick and Rayen Avenues. No indexing was recorded for newspaper articles in the Telegram and indexing didn't begin for the Vindicator until 1919. So, starting with both newspapers beginning January 1910, I searched page-by-page looking for articles on Scouting of yesteryear, going through hundreds of rolls of microfilm.

I went through countless boxes and documents at the Mahoning Valley Historical Society and conducted many interviews.

Information was then categorized, files created, and all the photographs matched with filed information in order to date and label them.

It has been an enjoyable experience. A journey I will remember.

Tony Valley Jr, 1960

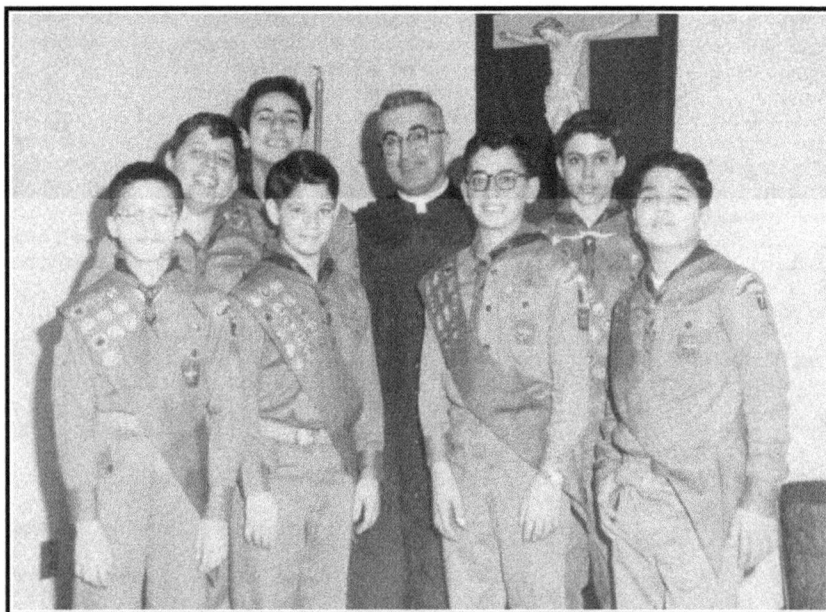

St. Anthony Troop #7 Altar Boys, 1962. Front row: (from left) Rocco Adduci, Tony Valley, Anthony Mancino, John D'Urso. Back row: Eugene DeGeorge, Michael Tomaskovich, Fr. Fred Anzivino, and Michael Addeo. (photo by Tony Ricci).

The first members of St. Anthony's Troop #7 when the troop started in October of 1959. Front row: (from left) Eugene Thomas, Anthony Valley Jr, Angelo Sorvillo, Anthony Mancino, John D'Urso, Michael Bodnar, Larry Drombetta Jr, Joseph Palermo, John Vogrin Jr, Billy Ceroli, Jerry Carelly, Salvatore Pizzulo, Tony Virgalitte, Darrly Dombroski, Frank Marsco, Rocco Adduci. Back row: Michael Addeo, Eugene DeGeorge, Philip Sisk, James Zarlenga, John Sabella, Jerome Dietz, Michael Tomaskovich, Senior Patrol Leader Joseph Menelle, Assistant Scoutmaster Sam Addeo, Scoutmaster Larry Drombetta Sr, Junior Assistant Scoutmaster Duffy Vialante, Edward Byrdy, John Cafaro Jr, Joe Fercana, Anthony Pizzulo, and Carl Dominic. Members not present: Felix Carmello, Jim Frank, Anthony Cicatiello, and Anthony Casciano. (photo by Tony Ricci).

1990 Summer Camp Staff at Camp Stambaugh. Standing on ramp: (from left) Angie Colon (K), Sandy Romano (AC), Todd Shaffer (K), Aunt Clara Casale (HC), Mark Vaughn (D), and Ed Dull (S). Kneeling on ramp: Tony Garcia. Front row: Ryan Day (C), Dave Starkey (C), Matt Bennett (C), Gordon Kieger (C). Second row: Mike Scott (A), John Starkey (S), Jeff Cepin (A), Rich Tunison (AR), Adam Doyle (SD), Aaron Bowser (L). Third row: Tony Valley (CD), Paul Iden (CO), Steve Cooper (A), Mike Kelley (CL), Ron Lodwick (ED), Tom Dunlap (AD), Mark Hradil (PD). Back row: Marvin Merritt (F), Steve Simmons (E), Ross Lucarell (CR), Wally Fowles (V), Bob Wilson (SSD), Ron Clark (S). Others not pictured: Dale Beckman (Trading Post Manager), Dominic Lucarell (Assistant to Camp Ranger), Terry Lee Mock (Trading Post), Rich Butterworth (L), Rob Keslar (A). (photo by Jack Acri). Letter codes: (A) Aquatics, (AC) Assistant Cook, (AD) Aquatics Director, (AR) Archery, (C) C.I.T., (CD) Camp Director, (CL) Clerk, (CO) Commissioner, (CR) Camp Ranger, (D) Dining Hall Steward, (E) Ecology/Conservation, (ED) Ecology/Conservation Director, (F) First Aid, (HC) Head Cook, (K) Kitchen, (L) Lake, (PD) Program Director, (S) Scoutcraft, (SD) Scoutcraft Director, (SSD) Shooting Sports Director, (V) Volunteer.

(1-2) Council Recognition Dinner, April 1990, with (1) Betty and Henry Sforza (left), and parents, Dorothy and Tony Valley Sr. (photo by Nick Valley). (2) Nick and Maria Valley. (photo by Tony Valley Sr.) (3) Cutting firewood in Camp Stambaugh, February 1988. Bill Cann (brother-in-law), Nick Valley, Jeff Dyer, Tony Valley (sitting). (4) Dominic Valley's Eagle Court of Honor, July 1976. Grandma Valley Anzivino, Dorothy, Dominic, and Tony Valley, and Nana Ripa. (5) With my bugle at Fr. Kanes Camp, Catholic Retreat Camporee, September 1966. (6) Council Recognition Dinner, May 1976. Wood Badgers Murle McLaughlin, Ray Slaven, Dr. Jack LeBrun, Tony Valley, Michael Balaban, Steve Seifert, and Walter Fowles.

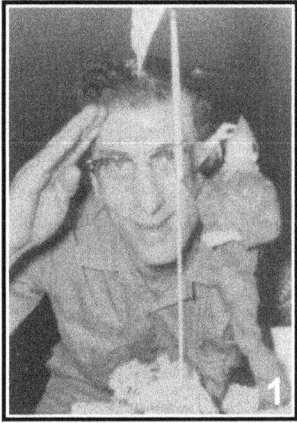

(1) Larry Drombetta, 1966. The first Scoutmaster of Troop #7. (2) Alex Seka, 1987. You never saw him without his camera. (3) David Wrikeman and Toby, 1970. Dave was also known as Paul Bunyan. (4) Joe Angelo, 1988. (5) Dominic Valley, 1990. (6) Book on map and compass I prepared in 1977 for training my Philmont groups. (7) John Wolboldt in 1987 with a Stambaugh beanie. (8) Murle McLaughlin, 1976. (9) Nick Valley at his Eagle Court of Honor, April 1967. (10) Bill Hunt in his mountain man outfit, 1989. (11) Fred Baird as District Executive of Pioneer District at a 1976 Annual District Dinner. (12) Mari Ann Valley Cann, 1988. (13) At Philmont's Tooth of Time in 1988. (14) 1991 Summer Camp patch design showing the four major areas in camp. The letters T.P. represent the designers, Tony (Valley) and Penny (Shaffer).

(All photos by author).

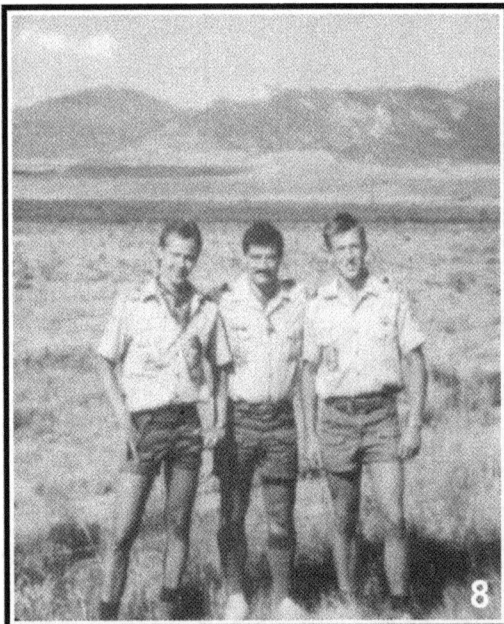

(1) Fr. Richard Maro, 1989. Was a member of Troop #7 and remained active in Scouting in Youngstown and Canton. (2) While posing for this photo in June of 1990, Bart Ingram and Tony Valley (back) hold rabbit ears over Don Ruse and Wally Fowles. They didn't know about the rabbit ears until now! Wally served as Camp Business Manager for many years and the other three served as Camp Directors. (3) Assistant Council Executive Bennet Taylor, 1977. (4) Joe Angelo at the Pioneer District Fall Camporee in 1976 with his black coffee pot. He never left home without it. (5) Jean Slaven, 1976, member of the Council Office Staff. (6) Camp chapel, winter of 1974. Katschke Lodge is in background and dining hall is on right. (7) 1967, Troop #7 Committee Chairman Tony Valley Sr, troop Treasurer John Cafaro, and past Scoutmaster Larry Drombetta. (8) Joe Metzger (left) and Tom Presby (right) from Troop #44 with Tony Valley in Philmont 1986. Tooth of Time is in background.

(9) Tony Valley makes a presentation to Scoutmaster Henry Sforza on behalf of Troop #7 during the troop's 25th Anniversary in 1984. (10) 1972, Troop #7 Scouts. Front: Lou Filaccio, Bill Huey, Vince Altieri, and Bobby Huey. Back: Dom Valley, Henry Sforza Jr, and Joe Giampietro. (11) New dining hall, 1993. It was built on the Moyer Health Lodge site. (12) Troop #7 Scouts, Tony Valley, Eugene DeGeorge and John Vogrin demonstrating first aid at a roundtable meeting in 1966. (13) National Camping School Aquatic Staff in Indiana, 1992: Steve Terrell, Tony Valley, Glen Schalk, Course Director Pat Noak, and Joel Shilling. (14) 1967 Troop #7 Eagle Court of Honor for Pete (left) and Gene (right) Drombetta. In center are parents Larry and Joann. (15) Lodge Advisor Tony Valley and Jeff Dyer, 1978. (16) Eagle Cabin (Neff's), 1993. (17) Mrs. Ted Parker and Thetas Smith, 1986.

(photos by the author).

87

TROOP #101's 50th ANNIVERSARY, November 1990. Front row: Marcus Harris, Sean Thompson, Joe Gaal, Matt Johnson, Eli Sears, Jason Bell, Robby O'Hara, Joe Thomas. Second row: David Starkey, Dan McCoy, Keith Johnson, Derek Bell, Ryan Cepin, Jim Majzun, Kevin Brodnan, Michael Dunn. Back row: Senior Patrol Leader Joe LoBoy; Assistant Scoutmasters: Merrill Harris, Jeff Cepin, Jack Bokesch, and Bill Mauch; Michael Scott; Jason Bokesch, Shaun Uscianowski; Scoutmaster John Holderman. Not present: Michael Shirilla, John Starkey, and Erik Hunter. (photo by author).

SECTION VI

Bugler Gene Maffei of Troop #150, Lynn-Kirk Church of Christ, at a Camporall in June, 1962. (photo by Vindicator).

MAPS

CAMP STAMBAUGH PROPERTY

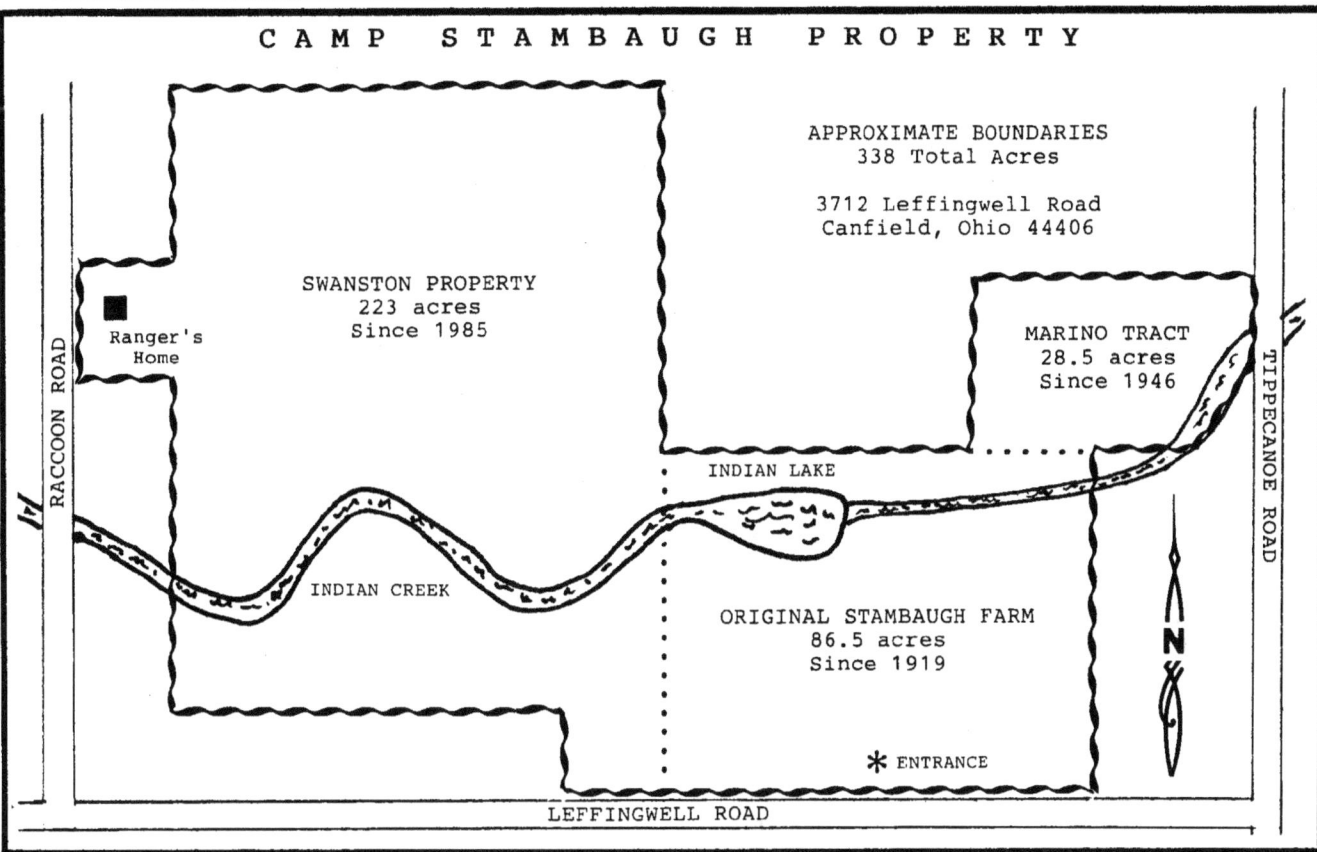

APPROXIMATE BOUNDARIES
338 Total Acres

3712 Leffingwell Road
Canfield, Ohio 44406

SWANSTON PROPERTY
223 acres
Since 1985

■ Ranger's Home

MARINO TRACT
28.5 acres
Since 1946

RACCOON ROAD

TIPPECANOE ROAD

INDIAN LAKE

INDIAN CREEK

ORIGINAL STAMBAUGH FARM
86.5 acres
Since 1919

N

* ENTRANCE

LEFFINGWELL ROAD

COUNCIL TERRITORY
Before and After Consolidation, February 10, 1993

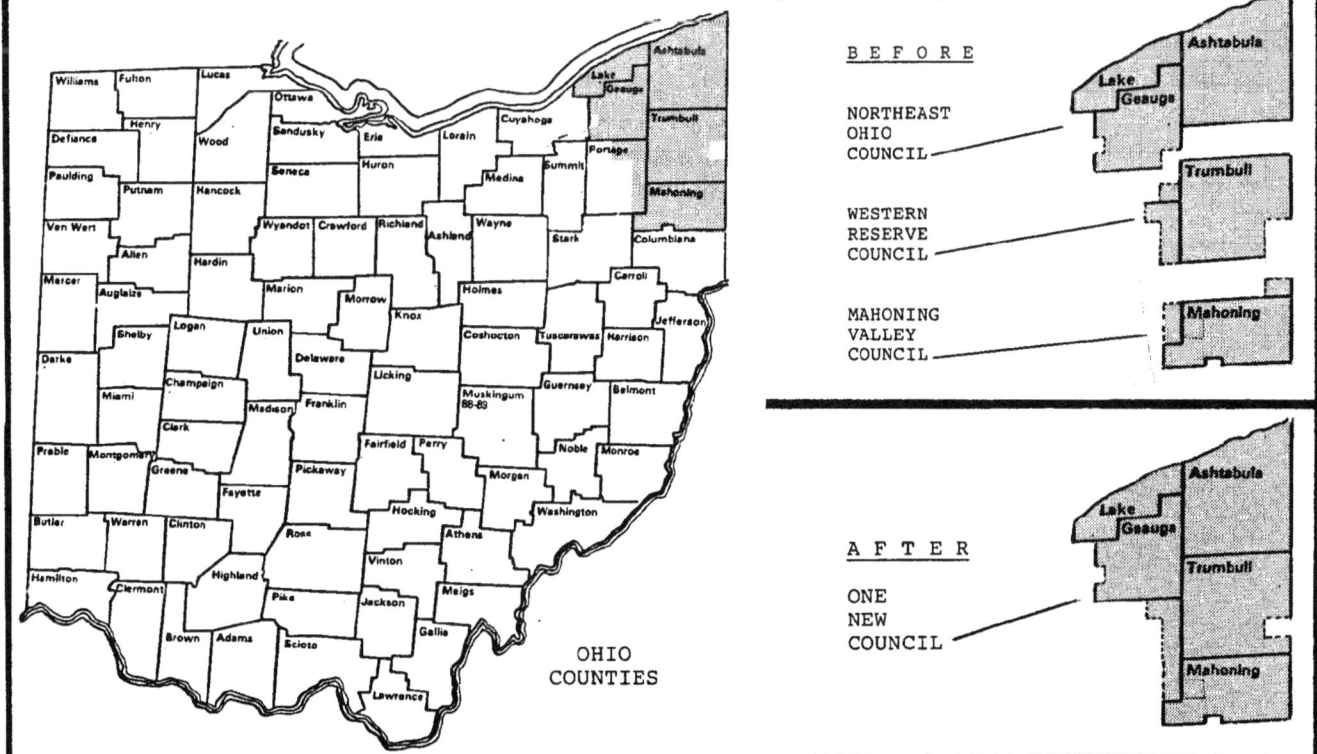

Williams, Fulton, Lucas, Ottawa, Sandusky, Erie, Lorain, Cuyahoga, Lake, Geauga, Ashtabula, Trumbull, Henry, Defiance, Wood, Seneca, Huron, Medina, Summit, Portage, Mahoning, Paulding, Putnam, Hancock, Wyandot, Crawford, Richland, Ashland, Wayne, Stark, Columbiana, Van Wert, Allen, Hardin, Marion, Morrow, Knox, Holmes, Carroll, Jefferson, Mercer, Auglaize, Logan, Union, Delaware, Licking, Coshocton, Tuscarawas, Harrison, Shelby, Champaign, Madison, Franklin, Muskingum 88-89, Guernsey, Belmont, Darke, Miami, Clark, Montgomery, Greene, Fayette, Pickaway, Fairfield, Perry, Noble, Monroe, Morgan, Preble, Warren, Clinton, Ross, Hocking, Washington, Butler, Hamilton, Clermont, Highland, Pike, Vinton, Athens, Meigs, Brown, Adams, Scioto, Jackson, Gallia, Lawrence

OHIO COUNTIES

BEFORE

NORTHEAST OHIO COUNCIL

WESTERN RESERVE COUNCIL

MAHONING VALLEY COUNCIL

Ashtabula, Lake, Geauga, Trumbull, Mahoning

AFTER

ONE NEW COUNCIL

Ashtabula, Lake, Geauga, Trumbull, Mahoning

90

INDEX

Information regarding camp refers to Camp Stambaugh unless otherwise noted.

Names of people and other information listed in the following categories are not recorded in this index.

NOTES & AUTOGRAPHS

www.ingramcontent.com/pod-product-compliance
Lightning Source LLC
LaVergne TN
LVHW081319060426
835509LV00015B/1586